W9-BPA-386

PETER LINDBERGH

GALLIANO

GALL

WEIDENFELD & NICOLSON

COLIN McDOWELL

IANO

IRVING PENN

'My role is to seduce'

I

DIOR:
Succès fou

HAUNTED BY ITS APPARENT INSTABILITY, the fashion world compensates by taking itself very seriously. Conscious of the accusations of fatuity levelled at it, afraid of its own volatility, unsure of whether it is art, commerce or craft, it searches desperately for historical moments with which to anchor itself.

And it finds them: 1860, when the Englishman Worth was appointed to dress the Empress Eugénie of France and, incidentally, to found the modern world of high fashion and the cult of the mystique of the couturier; 1918, when Madeleine Vionnet showed her four-pointed dress and gave the art of dressmaking a new dimension with her experiments in cutting cloth on the bias; Mary Quant's 1955 opening of her shop, Bazaar, on the King's Road, which heralded a fashion revolution that brought the needs of the young and the casual into the fashion equation for the first time. There are others, but the fashion moment generally considered the most historic of all was specific and precise: 12 February 1947 at 10.30.

It was the moment that was, at least temporarily, to change fashion with a suddenness never previously seen, and to set it on a course that proved irresistible to women, despite initial shock, hostility and public condemnation on the highest level. On 12 February Christian Dior's 'New Look', rumoured for weeks in Paris, became a fact.

Right: An evening dress for Christian Dior haute couture, spring/summer 1997, designed by John Galliano, appears to be as delicate as a butterfly's wing, but its gossamer lightness relies on an armature which is a complex mixture of geometry and engineering. (Photo: Sarah Moon, 1997)

Previous page: photo: Lauren van der Stockt, Christian Dior archive.

10

The story screamed around the world. Instantly, the New Look was a scandal, an outrage, unbelievably insensitive, totally impractical. But it was also news, in a way that fashion had never been before. What had Christian Dior – mild-tempered, shy and sensitive – done to create so much fuss? Nothing more alarming than to put back the clock seven years, to where it had stopped at the beginning of the Second World War. But he had done so with a sense of style and a theatrical extravagance that made all other fashion suggestions look *démodé*. The New Look – sloping shoulders, wasp waists, padded hips and big skirts – was so convincing a statement that, within three seasons, not only were the world's couturiers following Dior's lead, but the look was also already being worn by ordinary women, to whom such extreme fashions had seemed ludicrous when they first appeared.

A moment like that will never be seen again. Fashion has moved from the autocratic base upon which it rested in those days, when French couture dictated how all fashionable women would dress. Now there is no consensus: Paris must fight for supremacy against Milan, New York and even London; and within all fashion capitals designers project widely different ideas of how women should dress, from the pared-down efficiency of minimalism and sportswear seen in New York and the eccentric eclecticism of London's fashion, to the richly wearable clothes of the Italian designers

In 1947, the 'Bar' suit was considered perfectly to encapsulate the spirit of the New Look. In 1997, John Galliano retains the New Look's confidence and glamour while adding sex, the modern fashion ingredient. (Drawing, left: Rene Gruau; right, Christian Dior spring / summer 1997 designed by John Galliano. Photo: Christian Dior archive)

and the darkly complex creations of the Japanese. Even when a certain place or time seems to encapsulate the mood of the moment, there are always maverick designers who fit into no accepted scheme: Isaac Mizrahi and Geoffrey Beene in New York; Christian Lacroix and Rei Kawakubo in Paris; Giorgio Armani and Moschino in Milan; Jasper Conran and Vivienne Westwood in London. There are few points of contact in today's fashion and, therefore, no possibility of a dominant force emanating from one designer alone, as with the New Look.

That does not mean the end of historic moments per se. They will continue to happen as long as young talent is permitted to bid for its place in the sun. One such moment occurred in January 1997, when John Galliano created his first collection as chief designer of the house of Dior.

It was an emotional occasion and, many would claim, a significant one. It marked not only the fiftieth anniversary of the New Look, but also the creative coming-of-age of John Galliano, a designer who had never failed to be controversial, and who had become a world-class figure in the years since he had graduated from St Martin's School of Art, London, in 1984.

Galliano's appointment to the most august fashion house in Paris had taken some commentators by surprise. Amidst all the rumours that sprang up on the announcement that the Italian designer Gianfranco

Creating couture clothes is a painstaking and time-consuming process which has hardly changed since Dior's day, but the efforts are all worth it in the final joy of a job well done. (Photo, left: Lauren van der Stockt; above, photo: Bellini, both courtesy, Christian Dior archive)

Ferré, who had designed the Dior collection since 1990, would not be continuing, few had seriously considered Galliano. It had seemed unlikely that he would be offered the job at Dior because only a year had elapsed since he had taken up his appointment as designer at Givenchy. Like Dior, Givenchy is part of the huge luxury conglomerate, Louis Vuitton Moët Hennessy, formed in 1987 by Bernard Arnault – the man who had placed Galliano at Givenchy and would now make the appointment at Dior.

In fact, Arnault had been negotiating Galliano's move to Dior for much of the time that Galliano had been at Givenchy. 'It was a great strain,' the designer says now. 'I couldn't tell anybody, not even my closest collaborators. I was sworn to absolute secrecy and had to go on as if nothing was happening. It was a lonely, stressful time but, in the end, it was worth it.'

Indeed it was. After years of financial uncertainty, John Galliano had been handed Paris fashion's golden apple. All he had to do was succeed. But it was not entirely clear what kind of success Bernard Arnault was looking for. The house of Dior might well be the most famous fashion establishment in the world (although most would feel that it must share that honour with Chanel – another house trading on a past based on one of the great fashion personalities, but kept vibrant by

Karl Lagerfeld's bold, iconoclastic approach to modern fashion – or even the house of Saint Laurent, whose eponymous designer still managed to please and impress a large section of the fashion world). However, it had not commanded Paris since it had sacked Yves Saint Laurent, Dior's personal choice as his successor, in 1960. Arnault knew that, if the huge publicity potential of the fiftieth anniversary of the New Look were not to be thrown away, he had to choose someone who could put the spirit back into the house of Dior.

Paris felt that he would choose Jean-Paul Gaultier, a maverick guaranteed to command considerable journalistic interest. London favoured Vivienne Westwood, the notorious self-publicist who had frequently expressed her admiration of Christian Dior as a creator and a craftsman. Yet Arnault saw a potential for originality and growth in John Galliano that was not apparent in the other two – nor, indeed, in any other names mentioned in the succession hiatus.

History repeats itself in fashion as in any other field. Before being offered his own house by the textile billionaire Marcel Boussac, Christian Dior had been given the opportunity to revive the moribund Paris fashion house, Maison Philippe et Gaston, founded in 1925, which in pre-war Paris was still reasonably successful. Bought by Boussac in 1946, it had not fared well during the war, and, when Dior went to look at it

in 1946, it was sadly reduced in name (and became known only as Gaston) and output (concentrating almost exclusively on furs). Above all, as Dior immediately realized, the firm's aura was hopelessly old-fashioned. In his own words, he recognized 'the impossibility of adding new wine to old bottles in a trade where true originality is all-important… I decided that I was not meant by nature to revive the dead.'

Not that there was any question for Galliano of reviving the house of Christian Dior from the dead. After Saint Laurent's exit, it had enjoyed years of quiet prosperity with Marc Bohan as its design director. Under his guidance, it had managed to retain more couture customers than any other Paris house. Under his successor, Gianfranco Ferré, it had maintained not only respectable sales, but also a respectable profile. In a sense, this was what worried Arnault. He did not want anything respectable for the anniversary of the house of Dior. He was looking for outrage, excitement, publicity and profile on the level enjoyed by Dior in 1947.

It was more complicated even than that. Whereas other contenders for the job would certainly garner publicity, it would be of the wrong sort. Westwood and Gaultier would scandalize and, inevitably, alienate. Others might be tempted to recreate the actuality of the New Look and miss the modernity he clearly wished the house to project. To work with originality in tune with the spirit of another creator while keeping

Christian Dior took much of his New Look inspiration from the days when his mother was young. Galliano also takes the hour-glass figure – surely the most alluring female silhouette since the Minoans – and reinvents the Edwardian look in totally contemporary terms for Cleo, a bustier sheath dress of lilac taffeta overlaid with lace, a jet choker and a Masai corset. (Left: Harlingue-Viollet; right, photo: Michel Nafziger, courtesy L'Officiel, *Paris, March 1997)*

your own handwriting clear is to walk on a creative knife's edge. Only the most sensitive, tactful and self-assured can have any hope of success. It was because he felt that John Galliano had this rare combination that Arnault offered him Dior.

Recreating history is not easy, nor is it required. Galliano's task was to make his own historic statement and, in order to do that, he sought out the essence of the Dior style. On 21 October 1996, at 10 o'clock, Galliano had his first appointment with Soizic Pfaff at 18 bis, rue Jean Goujon, just around the corner from the Dior headquarters in rue François 1er. Soizic was nervous. Although she had worked for Dior for some years, she had only been appointed archivist three weeks earlier. Would she be able to help the designer in the way she felt an archivist should?

The archive at rue Jean Goujon forms a fascinating adjunct to the vast Christian Dior machine at François

1er. It consists of one rather dark and hopelessly over-crowded room, the antithesis of glamour and hardly the setting for efficiency. But it contains everything anyone looking for the spirit of Dior could require. A long, deep room, one of its walls is entirely taken up by a built-in cupboard that contains the dresses from Christian Dior's time – or, at least, a good selection of them. Some are originals that have always been in the house, others are copies of key garments from his *œuvre*; many have been donated by their original clients, others bought at sales and from dealers around the world.

The remaining walls contain shelves full of books of original sketches and photographs of the creations designed for Dior's twenty-two collections. With few gaps, every dress and *tailleur* is recorded. In many cases, the record consists of a photograph taken in the atelier, showing the front and back of the garment.

The lure of pre-revolutionary China has a powerful effect on John Galliano. There is a stillness and a fluidity in his dresses recreated under the influence of heroines like Anna Marie Wong, Gertrude Lawrence and, inevitably, Dietrich in Shanghai Express. *(Photos: Jean-Marie Perier,* Elle, *Paris, February 1997)*

For his first Dior collection, Galliano took the original spirit of the house with wit and tact by bringing his own vision to Christian Dior's 'trademark' details. (Below left, photo: Mike de Dulmen, 1957, Christian Dior archives; below right: 1954, Christian Dior archives)

Below left, Christian Dior archives; below right, Christian Dior prêt-à-porter, autumn/winter 1997–8, designed by John Galliano, photo: Christian Dior archives.

These are not glamorous fashion photographs, but 'bread-and-butter' images to record the appearance rather than the spirit of the item. Most garments are also represented by a drawing. Simple, linear and concentrating on shape rather than detail, these were produced in the atelier on press handouts.

In Dior's time, the dissemination of high fashion was far different from today. There were no designer labels, as such, and the nearest a couturier got to ready-to-wear was the range of sports and beach wear which he sold in his boutique – if, indeed, he bothered to have one. The items had nothing in common with his couture collection and were never designed by the

Dior enjoyed creating monumental shapes. Galliano translates the spirit of a sculpted evening gown by taking the inspiration of its deep, almost architectural folds to make his own statement.

maestro himself. He concentrated entirely on his couture collections, shown in January and July.

Primarily for private customers and the representatives of the world's most exclusive stores and private labels, the couture shows were shrouded in secrecy – necessarily so. There was an embargo on photographs of the clothes appearing in the press for at least six weeks after the show so that orders from customers could be executed before the impact of their novelty was dulled by press coverage. This was important for private clients, but even more important for such stores as Saks Fifth Avenue or Harrods, who bought the right to sell line-for-line copies of the original models, either under their own label, or that of the designer – in which case materials and trimmings had to be identical with those on the original model shown at the collection.

The fear was piracy. If a pirate firm – which had not proved its *bona fides*, had not been present at the collection and had not paid the considerable premium required for the right to reproduce the designs – managed to get its copies out first, it could clearly ruin the market of those who had taken the correct – and expensive – route. Because no photographer was allowed near a couture show in those days – Dior himself personally ejected a client who was discovered with a miniature camera hidden in her hat – drawings for the press, giving the minimum of detail, were an essential part of a couture house's service. It is these drawings which are held at 18 bis.

And it was these, along with the photographs, that initially excited John Galliano and his assistant, Steven Robinson. They had come to do their homework – a crash course in discovering the spirit of Dior and, as Soizic Pfaff recalls, they wanted to see everything. The

Below left: autumn/winter 1948–9, Christian Dior archives; below, Christian Dior prêt-à-porter, autumn/winter 1997–8, designed by John Galliano. (Photo: Frédéric Garcia, Christian Dior archive)

books of photographs and drawings began to sprout hundreds of yellow stickers as the men truffle-hunted through the archive. Although primarily interested in the designs created by Dior himself, they also looked at those by Saint Laurent and many of the early ones of Bohan. Soizic made hundreds of photocopies.

Determined to get the whole picture, Galliano worked in the archive for an entire week. Not satisfied, he came in for a weekend and an extra Saturday. At night he borrowed books on Dior and videos of Ferré's shows. Soizic's initial fears had been quickly dispelled. When she told Galliano how briefly she had held the job, he said, 'That makes two of us. Don't worry, we'll learn together.' She recalls how his enthusiasm never waned, even at the end of long days in the stuffy room. 'It was fascinating,' she says. 'He was so excited. He wanted to see everything. Old newspaper cuttings, press books and all the little details.'

Two of the most precious books – because they are the only ones to survive – are the *Livres de Fabrication* from 1947 and 1948, which give the technical specification of each garment in the show. A small sketch and brief description are followed by a detailed listing of materials used, the name of the garment and the names of the people responsible for making it. For example 'Bar', the most famous of all the creations shown in the first collection, was a *tailleur* consisting of a jacket in shantung and a skirt in wool. The jacket alone required 3.75 metres of shantung and 3 metres of lining. It was cut by Pierre Cardin, who worked for Dior before he opened his own establishment. (It was traditional for jackets to be cut by men and skirts to be cut by women – in this case, Monique.)

If John Galliano found such details fascinating, he found the charts that detailed the name of the garment,

for the major Dior retrospective mounted to coincide with the fiftieth-anniversary celebrations. The best of the rest were required for 'Christian Dior Spirit', a spectacular one-evening-only show arranged by Katell le Bourhis and Gianfranco Ferré for the Dior Gala on 9 December in New York. As the new designer for Christian Dior, John Galliano was present at the gala and, as Soizic Pfaff says, 'He clearly worked when he was in New York. He came back wanting to see even more details.'

The search for the spirit of Dior was almost complete.

But there were two more vital pieces required to complete the picture. Of one, John Galliano was aware. The other was to be a serendipitous discovery.

Les Signes de Reconnaissance de la Maison Christian Dior is a thick, spiral-bound book for use only within the company. It isolates the components that make up the style of the house of Dior, dealing with the fabric and furnishing of the house: the colours, textures and inspirations of Dior, and the accessories and publicity which add strength to the griffe, or label. It is, perhaps, an analysis that could be made by anyone who bothered to take the time to examine the house set up by Dior, but it is an invaluable and speedy form of induction for the tyro in the firm.

Starting with the famous grey-and-white colour scheme based on the Louis XVI period, chosen by Dior for its simplicity, sobriety and classicism, as well as for its cool elegance that bespoke Paris for him, *Les Signes de Reconnaissance* examines the components of the décor of Avenue Montaigne. Created for Dior by Victor Grandpère, these include: the famous little gilt salon chairs with their wicker seats, the grey-and-white armchairs, the pearl-rimmed oval medallion

Left: Christian Dior, prêt-à-porter, autumn/winter 1997–8, designed by John Galliano: the lingerie look as catwalk motif. (Photo: Christian Dior archives)

its model, *vendeuse* and customer even more so. Above all, he found the swatches of material which were pinned to the charts deeply moving. He pored over colours and textures of fabrics left largely undisturbed for fifty years. He had discovered the essence of a Christian Dior creation – the raw material that excites, stimulates and challenges the true couturier.

And, of course, there was the joy of closely examining the made-up garment in the cupboard. The two men were not content merely to look and touch. They needed to analyse and itemize what made a Dior creation unique. Several key garments were taken to the studio in order for the designer to fully study them from every angle.

In this, Soizic had a problem. She felt she was letting them down because she had so few examples of *flou*, light dressmaking as opposed to tailoring, which created the spectacular ballgowns that were one of the strongest statements in Dior's collections during the fifties. Most of the really magnificent examples were in New York, on loan to the Metropolitan Museum of Art

DENTELLE MARINE

Robe Sirene
en Crepe Satin
Brillant
Avec dentelle
Noir

Robe
Bustier
avec 2ᵉ
Robe
en
Dentelle

Coupe en
Plein
biais

Fente Longue
en Coté
avec train
dos

Train

The first Galliano dress for Dior was a lingerie-look creation for the Princess of Wales (right), who was guest of honour at the Metropolitan Museum of Art, New York, in December 1996. Left: John Galliano's original sketch for the dress. (Photo, right: Rex Features)

containing the firm's logo, The book looks at Dior's favourite flowers – the rose and, pre-eminently, the lily of the valley, used as the basis for his perfume, Diorissimo, which was created by Edmond Roudniska in 1956 – and his colours: soft pinks, pearl greys – which Dior felt were 'très Paris' – reds, and 'glorious black', which he considered the supreme colour of elegance.

Dior divided fabrics into the masculine and feminine. The former, predictably enough, were largely what he called the 'English' fabrics: hound's-tooth check, Prince of Wales check and all the fabrics worn by the Duke of Windsor. (In Dior's day, the Duke was considered the archetypal British dandy, renowned for the Savile Row perfection of his appearance, even though his clothes were by no means all from the home of traditional sartorial elegance.) Above all, Dior loved pinstripes, the uniform of the English establishment, because for him, they symbolized *'l'élégance brittanique'*, which had always so impressed him.

The feminine fabrics were as French as the masculine were British. Crepe, tulle, organza and lace

A couturier's creativity is open to all stimuli and the decorative appeal of ethnic dress is considerable. However, it takes a strong imagination and a sure hand to avoid a result that might look patronizing. Galliano, here, adapts ethnic details to haute couture, avoiding all the pitfalls and retaining the powerful images of photographer Mirella Ricciardi, which are a continuing influence on John Galliano. (Left, photo: Peter Lindbergh; above: Mirella Ricciardi)

– both *dentelle* and *guipure* – were the basis of the soft fluidity of Dior's romantic day dresses and the medium of some of the most magnificent evening dresses created this century. In Dior's hands, they were used to unite femininity and grandeur in a memorably theatrical way. Even today, photographs of Dior's grand ballgowns of the fifties move us by their authority as much as their beauty. It isn't hard to imagine Galliano's excitement as he pored over the pages of *Les Signes de Reconnaissance*, especially when he knew that several superb examples hung in Soizic's long cupboards waiting to be examined with painstaking attention to detail.

*The Orient excited
Parisian aristic and social
circles from the late
nineteenth century up to
the 1920s. A hundred
years later John Galliano
follows in the footsteps of
Degas and Manet in his
recreation of a cultural
mood for Christian Dior's
Prêt-à-Porter
autumn/winter 1997–8
advertising campaign, on
which he worked as
creative director, with
photographer Nick Knight,
art director Peter Saville,
and model Shalom
Harlow. (Photo: Nick
Knight)*

Exciting as his discoveries were, none was especially surprising. But, in his researches into the final famous element in the Dior vocabulary, the leopard print first shown in 'Jungle', a day dress, and 'Africaine', a leopard-printed evening dress, on 12 February 1947 – and a feature of the Dior look from that moment – he discovered what was perhaps the most important element for him. His eye was arrested by a photograph taken by Cecil Beaton of a woman of supreme elegance, a woman of a certain age, a woman of total style. Wearing a leopard-skin coat, pushed slightly away from her shoulders to reveal a five-strand rope of pearls, with a leopard-skin turban with a veil, and sparkling diamonds at her wrist, she seemed the personification of the elegance of the house of Christian Dior for which John Galliano had been subconsciously searching.

The new young designer had discovered the legendary Mitzah Bricard. A woman of extravagant taste and extraordinary chic, totally cosmopolitan, a woman of the world, Germaine Bricard, always known as Mitzah, was, in Dior's own words, 'one of those increasingly rare people who make elegance their sole *raison d'être*'. She had worked in the thirties as a social and fashion adviser to Edward Molyneux, the British couturier in Paris renowned for his elegantly understated tailoring which, Dior admitted, had enormously influenced him. Originally appointed by Dior to oversee the millinery department – an area of extreme importance in the days when no *tailleur* was deemed complete without a chic hat – the influence of her taste went beyond hats, and informed the whole establishment. As Dior said, 'I knew that her presence in my house would inspire me towards creation.'

29

Leopard prints were a Dior trademark from his first show. Galliano gives them a completely new feeling by combining leopard with lace to produce a potent evening look: half-bedroom, half-jungle in its appeal. Nicole Kidman photographed by Karl Lagerfeld for Vanity Fair wearing a Christian Dior haute couture dress from the spring/summer 1997 collection designed by John Galliano. (Photos: above, Nepo, 1947, Christian Dior archive; right: Karl Lagerfeld)

*A design idea can be
recreated in many moods.
'Eloise' (right), created
by Christian Dior in 1948,
was revised by Marc Bohan
in 1980 as the source for
a spectacular orange cape,
and both were combined by
Galliano in 1997 to produce
'Kamata', a totally original
reworking of the theme. Left,
Christian Dior haute
couture, spring/
summer 1997, designed by
John Galliano (Photos: left,
Michael Thompson, Vogue,
Paris, March 1997 right:
Christian Dior archive)*

Mitzah Bricard's great contribution to Dior, apart from her impeccable taste, was the fact that she knew precisely how a woman should dress in order to please a man – which, in the forties and fifties, was the point and privilege of women who dressed at couture level. She had been one of the great courtesans of Paris in the interwar years, a successor to the *grandes horizontales* of the Belle Epoque and therefore a link with that period of 'figures muffled in furs, gestures *à la* Boldini, bird of paradise plumes and amber necklaces'. This was the period that had so enraptured Dior, together with the memories it stirred of his mother. It also entranced John Galliano and Steven Robinson in their search for a romantic ideal.

They fell in love with the idea of Mitzah Bricard as a distant but powerful muse, their imaginations fired by the tales of her stylish attitudes: how she had been the mistress of a Russian prince, who showed his infatuation by showering her with pearls; how she wore a scarf tied at her wrist to disguise the scar left after a suicide attempt in the early days when she was young and vulnerable. Above all, they were attracted by her superb *ex cathedra* comments, such as her dismissal of society women whom, she felt, had brought down the profession of the *demi-mondaine* because, 'They'll go to bed for a *café crème*'. This was all from a woman who spent her days either at Dior or in the Ritz and loathed the countryside – when asked who was her favourite florist, she unblinkingly replied, 'Cartier'.

Through her, Galliano and Robinson moved back to Dior's mother and the tightly waisted, elegantly shaped silhouettes of their favourite period: those marvellous years of the new century before the First World War when high life, for the grotesquely over-privileged and pampered, produced fashionable attitudes that lasted

long after the money and power that had originally sustained them had been swept away. It was the world of flash and dazzle; the world in which great jewellers such as Cartier thrived; the world when the grand hotels were at their grandest; the world where no discomfort was too great, provided the end result was *le dernier cri* of fashionable luxury. It was a world already known and loved by John Galliano through the paintings of John Singer Sargent and Boldini.

It was that world which connected him to the spirit of Christian Dior. At the end of his research with the archivist Soizic Pfaff, John Galliano was ready to create the collection which, while being as modern as he could make it, would be a romantic homage to the memory of Dior himself, and all of Dior's own memories in turn, which had given the famous

New Look collection such an impact in 1947.

But that wasn't all that 18 bis, rue Jean Goujon had revealed. While researching there daily John Galliano had begun to realize that he and Dior had much more in common than the new designer could have imagined when he had signed his contract with Bernard Arnault. Dior had been young in the twenties, when Paris was at the cutting edge of artistic excitement, a time of creative and sexual licence when young men could live their lives on a carefree level of hedonism with no one

'John is from the school of perfection where the stitching in the lining must be as perfect as the stitches that can be seen.'

— MANOLO BLAHNIK

For the Christian Dior prêt-à-porter autumn/winter 1997–8 collection designed by John Galliano, he chose softness and fluidity as the form of the moment, in this advertisement photographed by Nick Knight, with Galliano as creative director, Peter Saville as art director, and model Yasmeen Ghauri. (Photo: Nick Knight)

to moralize or attempt to interfere. John Galliano had been young in London in the eighties, a time of social and artistic freedom when, to many, sex and drugs and rock and roll had seemed a sufficient end in themselves. Dior had trawled the bars of Montparnasse, the rue Tronchet, the Tip Toes. Galliano was intimately acquainted with the clubs of Soho, Old Compton Street, the Beat Route and Taboo. Dior had known poverty. At the age of twenty-six, he had found himself in Paris with no home or money, reduced to sleeping on friends' floors. Galliano was frequently broke in the eighties, and also no stranger to the world of squats and friends' floors.

Both men were incurably romantic, loving the life of *La Bohème*; *La Dame aux Camélias*, and all the doomed beauties who brought men pleasure, no matter how briefly, before their lives were ended by consumption or starvation. They also adored the sort of women personified by Mitzah, the ones who survived and used men for their own ends, ruthlessly milking their wealth in the undying quest for perfection. They loved dressing up – Dior was never happier than when playing charades or attending an elaborate and costly fancy-dress ball. Even in middle age he vividly recalled the excitement of the annual costume ball held at the Casino in Granville, his home town in Normandy, when he was a teenager. Galliano adored clubbing which, in the eighties, meant dressing as outrageously as ingenuity and money would allow.

It all came down to a common link: theatricality.

That is why Galliano set about designing his first collection for Dior with such confidence. Shown in January 1997, it was his opportunity to prove that couture was not dead; that high fashion could look forward even while glancing back; that beauty and finesse were not confined to the dressing-up box of history. But although there was a feeling that he wished to revisit the glories of the Dior past, Galliano was also conscious of the glories of his own past. And he realized that, without new elements, homage collections could slip dangerously towards the borderline between cultural atavism and pastiche. He was aware that if his first couture collection was to have the right degree of modernity, it must contain other elements.

And it did. With a hand worthy of Dior himself, Galliano conceived a show of dazzling eclecticism that fully justified the programme note claim: 'The spirit is one of change.' To the drama of Boldini women; to the beauty of the famed Countess Morosini in Venice, admired by the Kaiser, who addressed his letters, which never failed to reach their destination, 'To the Most Beautiful Woman, in the Most Beautiful House, in the Most Beautiful City in the world', and the *cocottes* of pre-1914 Paris; to the mystery of China and the opium dens of the twenties; to Brooke Astor reminiscing about her childhood in Peking; to Marlene Dietrich and the *Shanghai Express*; to the Bricard animal prints and the Savile Row tailored fabrics; to all of these Galliano added the unexpected ethnic touch of Masai jewellery, which lifted the collection away from nostalgia and made it the most strongly directional statement of the fashion season.

And the direction was exactly parallel to that of Dior's first collection, fifty years previously: towards seduction. Galliano's concept of femininity was about woman as *femme fatale*, as huntress and heroine, proud of her sexuality and at ease with her power. Constantly, with tact and grace, references were made to the original vision of Dior as seen by the modern eyes of Galliano: 'Diorbella', a hound's-tooth suit in black and white with a 'Mitzah' lilac lining; 'Diorla', a sleeveless crepe dress in ivory. The first seventeen outifts, for '*Jour, Déjeuners et Voyages*', all had names that played on 'Dior' – including some awkward ones such as 'Gallidior' – to emphasize the link.

But it was the '*Fin d'après-midi*' and '*Soir, grands soirs et bals*' sections which showed that Galliano was master – of himself, of Dior and of Paris. The audience became increasingly excited as the models appeared: 'Kitu', a mermaid dress in flower-painted silk taffeta; 'Kimoja', a jungle-green bias-cut sheath under a spectacular multi-coloured parrot feather cape; 'Cleo', an Edwardian sheath of jet-embroidered lilac taffeta with a jet Masai corset; 'Mitzah', a lilac silk, tulle and organza evening gown in the grandest fifties manner, and, most spectacular of all, 'Kamata', a brilliant

orange and fire evening gown with trailing skirts and layers of petticoats worn with a Masai plate necklace and breastplate. Then, 'Paloma', the wedding dress that traditionally always ends any couture collection, in pleated white chiffon, organza feathers and bird heads, and it was all over, the long hours and many weeks of work, shown briefly and once only, in less than thirty-five minutes.

The Galliano for Dior couture show at the Grand Hotel had been spectacular. Conceived on a lavish scale, it was full of superlatives even without the clothes. Whereas other designers showed in the ballroom, the Dior show used most of the hotel's ground floor, which was turned into a facsimile of the décor of the Dior showroom in Avenue Montaigne, including its famous staircase on which luminaries such as Cocteau and Dietrich had been happy to sit in Dior's shows in the fifties. It was a lavish gesture calculated to impress the world with Bernard Arnault's confidence in his young protégé.

Clearly, money had been spent: 791 gold chairs were arranged in two rows so that all the guests were close enough to the models to feel as involved as they would have been in an original Dior show; the salons were decorated with magnificent flower arrangements using 4,200 roses; the walls were covered with 800 metres of grey Dior fabric. It had taken 146 people thirty-six hours to transform the hotel into a *maison de*

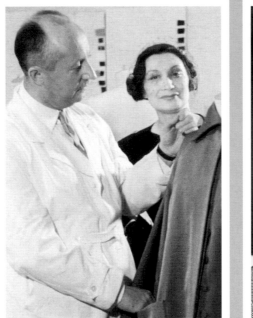

couture and, behind the scenes, 50 mannequins, 50 dressers, 16 hairdressers and 15 make-up artists had worked for over eight hours to make sure that every model looked totally perfect as she stepped out to face the crowd which, together with the gate-crashers, numbered well over a thousand.

In their number were fashion's movers and shakers, the editors of the great magazines, the fashion writers, the social commentators and the cream of Parisian social and political life, all of whom the house of Dior hoped would return to buy – as, indeed, many did. *Women's Wear Daily* reported that the day after the show, Dior's three couture salons had been filled to capacity with appointments from half-past eight in the morning to after seven o'clock at night, and Caroline Grouvel, Directrice de Couture, had been forced at times to allow fittings in her office, from which, in between, she reported that the bestsellers were the ballgowns, which were being ordered in white, to be worn as wedding gowns.

The press were equally as enthusiastic. *The New York Times* declared, 'Among Couture Debuts, Galliano's is the Stand Out', and continued, 'Mr Galliano's show was a credit to himself… to Mr Dior… and to the future of the art'. *Il Messaggero* claimed, 'Here in Paris, Fashion Speaks English.' *Women's Wear Daily* considered that, 'Galliano's Fashion Moment' had 'all the right ingredients: beauty,

direction and more than enough drama to keep the fashion flock in a tizzy', and the *International Herald Tribune*, praising Galliano's 'divine madness', said, 'Surely Galliano's 16-year career has been a dress rehearsal for this sublime moment?' Most extravagant of the accolades came two months later with the all-important collections issues of the great fashion magazines: Galliano's clothes featured on the front covers of the March issues of *French Vogue, Elle, Marie Claire* and *L'Officiel*, as well as *Time* magazine.

John Galliano had come home on what the *International Herald Tribune* called his 'indelible images of magic and romance'. As he appeared to take his curtain call in scenes that the London *Daily Mail* felt were 'a bit like a coronation', many in the audience, remembering the comment of his friend André Leon Talley on his appointment to the house of Givenchy – 'I don't think John is going to start wearing grey flannel double-breasted suits' – were surprised to see him wearing a suit in Dior Prince of Wales grey and a hat to cover his newly removed dreadlocks. It was John Galliano's personal homage to the man who had founded Maison Dior so brilliantly fifty years previously.

Christian Dior, together with Mitzah Bricard, the couturier's muse and a continuing inspiration to his successor, John Galliano, who stands in front of a Dior forme on his 36th birthday. (Left, photo: Bellini, Christian Dior archive; right, photo: Bertrand Rindoff and Frédéric Garcia, Christian Dior archive)

CLOSE-UP: Creating the Collection

IS IT BECAUSE JOHN GALLIANO felt so isolated when he went to school in England after the warmth and ubiquity of the extended family life of the Mediterranean that his fashion 'family' is so important to him? Certainly, he needs his collaborators to be close and deeply involved with everything he does. Jeremy Healy, his music guru, has been a friend for more than twelve years. Amanda Harlech was Galliano's imaginative right hand from 1984 until his move to Dior in 1996. She and her husband had frequently slept on the floor of John's first workroom in the East End. When working on a collection, she had brought along her babies and popped them on a shelf to play with bolts of fabric while she got on with the process which Galliano has described as 'making all the madness sublime'. When John moved to Paris, she commuted from the fastnesses of Shropshire, where she lived a life of unimpeachable rusticity, to help him reveal 'the beauty, line, grace, humility and outrage that is burning in his clothes'.

Amanda Harlech's notebook of a collection – both an aide-mémoire and an inspiration

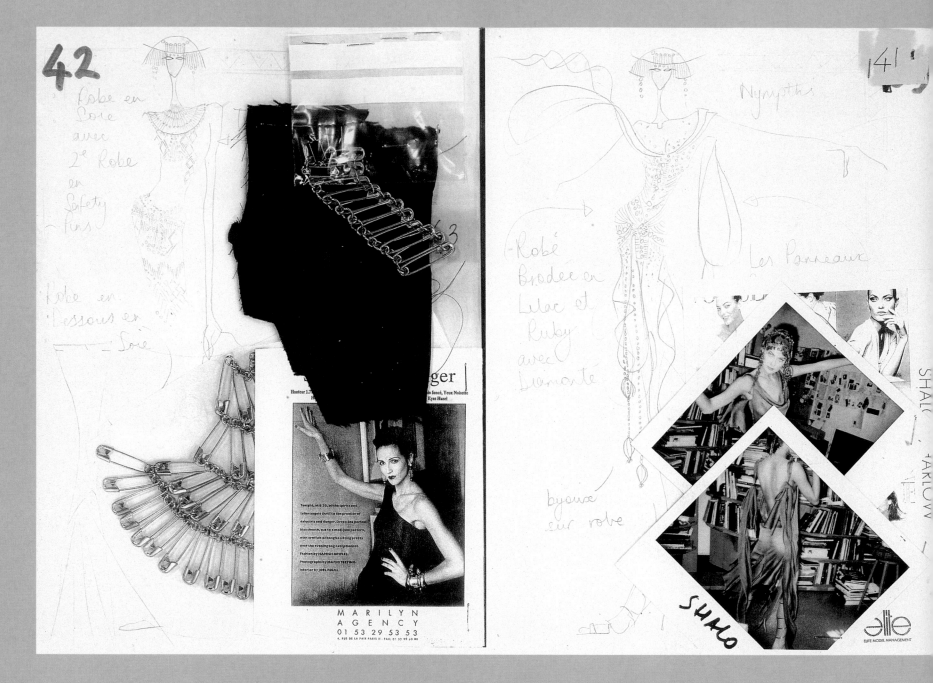

Sibylle de Saint Phalle, who began by modelling for him, remained by Galliano's side through the difficult London years and also joined him in Paris. Steven Robinson, who came to Galliano for a student placement in 1988, seems likely to remain with John for ever. He is so attuned to the designer that he is claimed by everyone, including John, to be his alter ego. Bill Gaytten, cutter and technical adviser, has been with John since the Fallen Angels collection, with only three years out in the mid-eighties. Collaborators cling to John Galliano.

The thing which cements them together is creative intensity. As Gaytten says, 'He is so imaginative. He gives you chances you wouldn't get anywhere else. You just have to look at the clothes to see that. They're not exactly Ralph Lauren. Where else would you get the chance to make a dress out of safety-pins – and not just cobbled together, but with all the passion that goes into any other dress?'

Just as every John Galliano show is a palimpsest of sources and stimuli, so every dress has a multi-layered history and speaks to fashion cognoscenti on several levels. According to Amanda Harlech, the original idea – for shows and collections – invariably comes from the designer. It can be something as inchoate as a colour, a

Couturiers are always ready
to take risks in order to push
fashion forward. For his own-
label, autumn/winter 1997,
prêt-à-porter collection
Galliano proved that shapely
and sophisticated garments
can be created from the
humblest of materials –
in this case safety pins.
(Photos: above, Patrice Stable
Agency; left, photos in John
Galliano's sketchbooks for his
prêt-à-porter autumn/winter
1997–8 collection include
ones by Mario Testino
and Irving Penn)

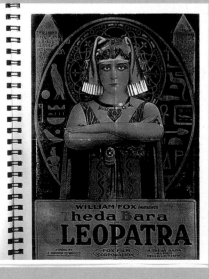

43

John Galliano's visual research ranges over many cultures and periods. Every item that interests him is collected in sourcebooks to be used as possible future stimuli. Intensely personal, they give a unique insight into the creative process which makes a Galliano collection a sophisticated multi-level statement.

All fashion designers are eclectic 'borrowers', throwing wide their nets in the search for inspiration. Galliano marshalls his ideas for a collection in sourcebooks which contain visual references of anything that has stimulated his imagination and will help to unfold the 'story' of his clothes.

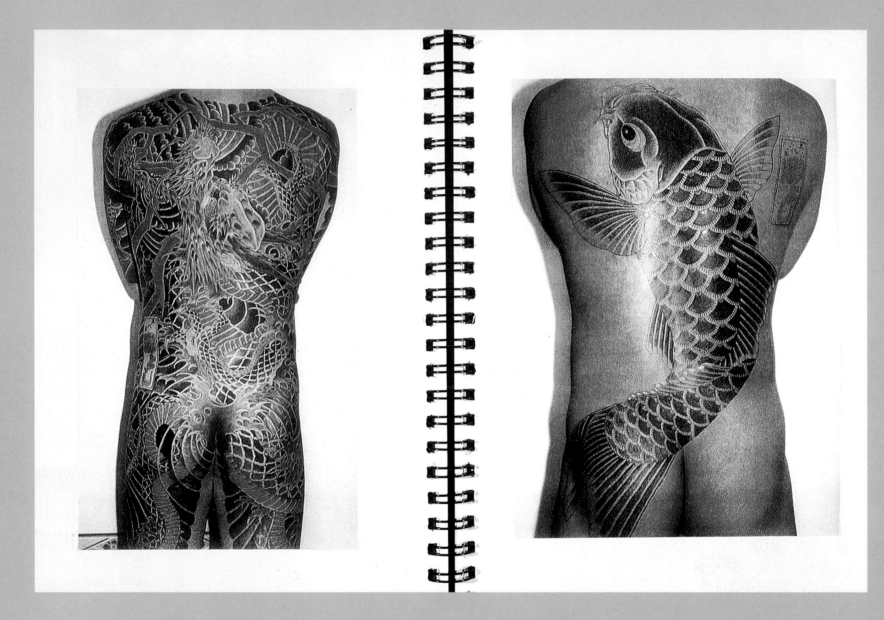

texture, or even one word for the imagination to latch on to. Steven Robinson says it can start to form as a story in John's head as much as a year ahead. 'It's a slow process,' he concedes. 'We don't all sit down and say, "Right, we've got to think of a story." Somehow, it all comes together naturally when we're researching.'

'John and I used to have endless conversations – often by telephone,' Amanda adds, "… What happens if she has a lilac velvet ribbon?"… " Yes, and black jet beading on the edge of the bodice"… "And she's in the forest, isn't she?"… "Yes, and… " They were marvellously exciting moments. And the story was always there, in John's head. And all the answers came out in the clothes. It's a question of ordering. It's like

stringing beads. That was my job really, helping to bring the beads together into a story necklace.' She refers nostalgically to 'the explorative joys of working with John. He was always the one who discovered the right painter or historic character as a basis for the story.'

Just as it is generally known that every Galliano collection has a story, whether for his own label or for Givenchy or Dior, it is no secret that he and his team spend considerable amounts of time in background research in order to create a world in which they can begin to design clothes. Much of the research is done in London. John and Steven spend a week at the beginning of each season steeping themselves in the

In the same autumn/winter 1997–8, prêt-à-porter show, tattoos and Egypt figure heavily as influences, which merge to create something entirely new. (Photos, right: Anthea Simms)

culture they know the best. As Steven says, 'More and more, we need to take in London. We visit London six to eight times per year, to get its spirit. We use the streets, the clubs, the libraries.' John explains further: 'We split London up by neighbourhood and then we leave ourselves entirely open. We always go to the markets – Camden, Portobello – and the V&A. We check out the bookshops and the exhibitions. Might go to the ballet or a musical. And we rely heavily on friends who can bring us into the picture and tell us what's what. Of course, there's clubbing – that's when I hook up with my old mates. I still party, but not as much as I did. In Paris, we're all working so hard that I have to lay the law down and say to the team, "Look, we *must*

47

The decorative extravagance of circus costume, especially when heightened by Hollywood's glamour machine, as in the 1952 film The Greatest Show on Earth, *starring Gina Lollobrigida as a tightrope artiste, is a rich source of inspiration for exotic decorative effects, including embroidery. (Right, for John Galliano, spring/summer 1997, Nadja Auermann wears a carousel horse Lesage embroidered silk tulle evening dress, photo: Niall McInerney)*

'He has a luminious quality which makes him unique in fashion: poetry, fantasy, magic, beauty – he dares to make us dream.'

– STEPHANE MARAIS

Icons of style and beauty feed the imagination of all couturiers. Givenchy's muse, Audrey Hepburn, was equally as inspiring for Galliano when he became design director for the house of Givenchy in 1995. (Photo: Andrew McPherson)

go out on Friday night. There's only four more Fridays before the collection!" But it has to be timetabled. Everything does now. A normal day starts at eight in the morning and can easily go on until ten at night. And there might be as many as twenty appointments in a day. I do ten collections a year. But London's different. I go with Jeremy on gigs. He takes me clubbing up north a lot now. Manchester… Liverpool… I love the clubs up there. They have a raw, driving energy. Very positive and strong. At the end of the week we come back to Paris with books, videos, antiques, old clothes – and minds buzzing with anticipation.'

Once their minds are ordered, John and Steven begin to build up the research books for the collection, creating pages from all the things which have stimulated them and totting up a visual storyboard. There will be postcards; photocopies; pages from books; pieces of fabric; Polaroids taken in museums or on the streets, scribbled notes by their side. The story does not always start with a woman, and the pages of the research book mix several atmospheres, cultures and historic eras. There are recurring themes, which often cross-reference with other collections, but the process is never formulaic.

'It's a very impressionistic approach,' John says. 'It's a dialogue between past and present. The starting point is usually factual, but we allow our imaginations to run riot. The story happens differently each time. Certain things begin to go around in my head and then we start to embroider on them. For example, the last Galliano show linked punk, Egypt and Theda Bara with uniforms and anti-establishment behaviour. And we kept getting coincidences. Somebody would say, "Did you know that Siouxsie Sioux of Siouxsie and the Banshees was obsessed with Theda Bara?" Then you think, "Oh! It's *so* right!" There's a story. So that's what you give to the team and they go off and do *their* research. They come back. "It was made of turquoise." "No it wasn't. It was lapis lazuli. I've checked. I went to the Louvre." All the time, the skeleton of the story is being clothed with layers of richness.'

The narrative once begun, different people get different parts of the tale. About six weeks before the show, John will say to Steven something like, 'There is this woman, born and bred in Russia and she runs away…' and then they're off. The story is taken up. 'This section needs to look like this,' gesturing to various pages in the research books. 'No, it needs to be

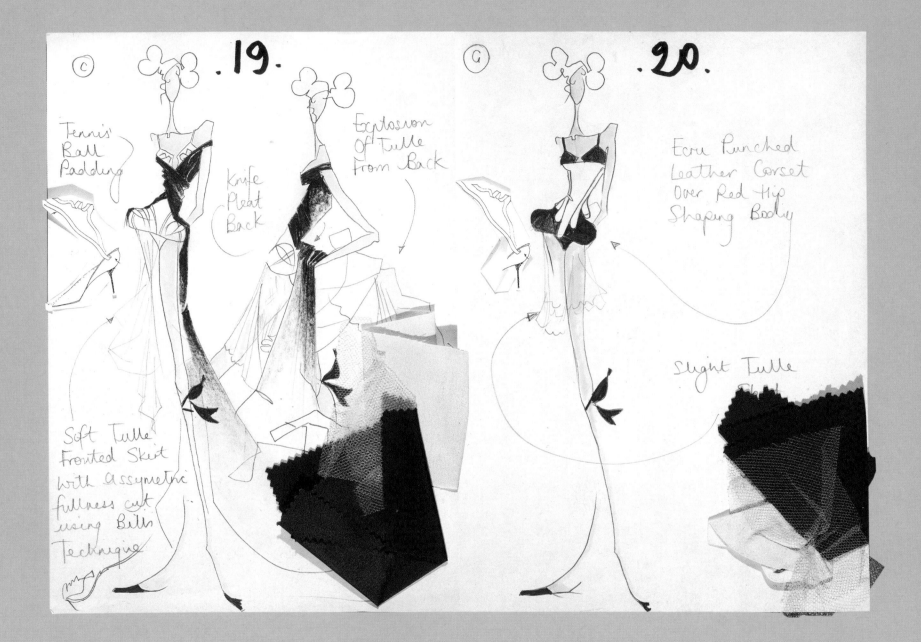

Writers have notebooks, composers music paper on which to work out their thoughts. For the dress designer it is a blank sheet of paper on which he formulates his ideas, but by the time the design is finalized it has become a crucial document, telling its own complete story.

As a collection takes shape, every outfit, identified by a number, is drawn with notes for the cutters in the atelier, along with fabric samples, Polaroids, or anything else which helps to bring the drawing towards the final three-dimensional creation – even the name of the model who will wear it.

more theatrical.' 'Well, *she* has to be theatrical. She's a screen goddess!' 'Its only a *B*-movie!' 'But she's given her all!' It sounds fun, even child-like, but this is a vital part of the creative chain – as Galliano says, 'It helps us to paint a rounded picture of the heroine and inspires us to develop the different looks in the collection.'

In the next stage John will call Jeremy and tell him the story. They won't discuss music at this point. It will be, 'This is how I'm beginning to feel about the collection.' Then drawings, photocopies, swatches and

Christian Dior
autumn/winter 1997,
designed by John Galliano
(Photos: Anthea Simms)

storyboards are sent over to London and Jeremy begins his research, working in much the way that John and Steven do, ranging as widely as possible over opera, eighteenth-century chamber music, jazz, rap and pop classics. He then mixes a test cassette to which John listens frequently and very attentively. The two men have worked closely for so many years that it is rare for John to reject anything, and soon the running order of the show is worked out in conjunction with the music. Steven believes that Jeremy's interpretation brings a vital element to the collection which sometimes makes John rethink certain things. Amanda Harlech agrees, saying that Jeremy Healey's input is vital: 'The music is like a multi-layered, rich, rich, rich carpet which mixes the savage and rarefied, as John's clothes do,' but she also adds, 'John has total faith in himself. Deep down, the core – the white heat, volcanic creativity – is all John's. Nobody can dampen that fire and, in a sense, that is what makes the rest rather unnecessary. It's *his* creative spark that matters. Of course, the team is important, but it is he who has the spark and the team hasn't.'

Inspired by the past, John Galliano makes a contemporary statement involving reworking the spirit of the original rather than slavishly copying its decorative forms. Shape and volume define a period more clearly than detail does. (Left: Givenchy haute couture, autumn/winter 1996–7, designed by John Galliano, photo: Paolo Roversi)

Nevertheless, as if to emphasize the coherence of the team, everyone involved admits that there is no such thing as a meaningful job description. 'Shared viewpoints mean more than job descriptions,' Vanessa Bellanger, Steven's assistant, insists. Of American and French parentage, she studied law and is able to bring attitudes not found in other members of the team. 'We are reference points for John,' she says. 'We're there to do whatever he needs to have done – which varies daily, even by the hour. It is a high-octane creative situation. You don't think about what your job is. You think, "What needs to be done?" Not for you. Not for your role. For John.'

He needs all the help available in order to prevent the pressure becoming too much. Even in between meetings and fittings there is almost always someone waiting for him to check something, or make a decision. In a sense, it is a self-imposed pressure, but a necessary one. As Steven Robinson points out, 'John controls everything, at every step. For instance, even though we've decided on shoe colours, John will check *every* shoe, down to the colour of the buckle. Nothing goes through until he has personally checked it – the buttons, the linings, *everything*. He goes into the atelier when everyone has gone home and personally checks. It's high-energy input from him all day.'

There is a basic structure to any collection. Even before designing begins, certain areas are pre-ordained. There must be day, cocktail, and evening wear, and that pattern underpins all creative

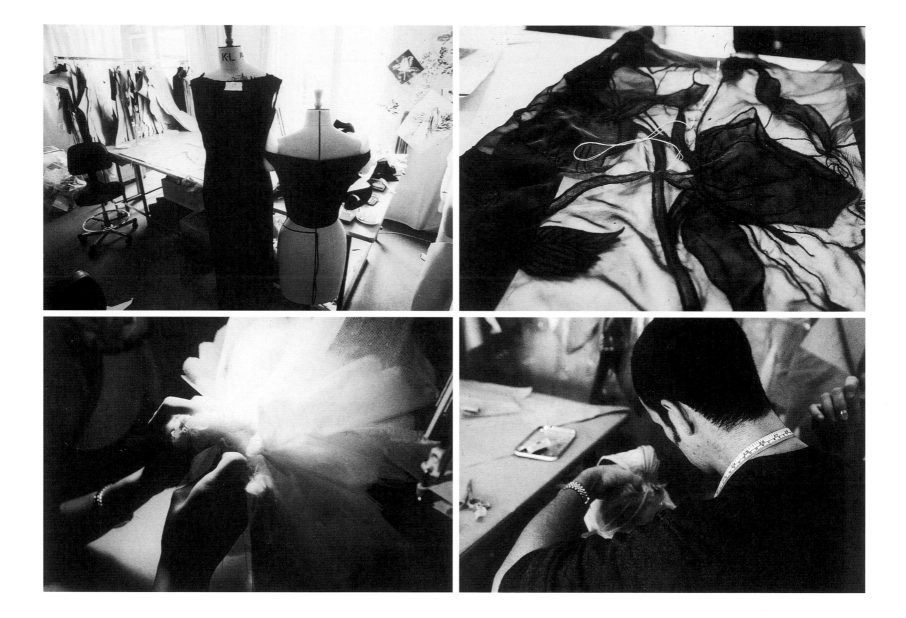

The glamour of a show is often belied by the hard work that goes on before, in these studio moments caught by Andrew McPherson during the preparations for John Galliano's spring/summer 1996 collection (Photos: Andrew McPherson)

The greatest inspiration for a couturier is fabric. Once he has that fixed in his mind his imagination is able to work in concrete terms. Without it a sketch is only a preliminary, abstract idea. It is how fabric works on the moving body that creates fashion.

thought-processes. As Galliano says, 'It's great to tell a story in a collection, but you must never forget that, despite all the fantasy, the thing is about *clothes*. And, all the time while you are editing to make the impact stronger, you have to remember that, at the end of the day, there has to be a collection and it has to be sold. We have to seduce women into buying it. That's our role. What you see on the runway isn't all that you get. That represents less than a quarter of what we produce. Merchandizing is vital. We have to keep the shops stocked, looking fresh and seductive. Markets need to be organized, and that takes time.'

As does the making of the dresses for the show. 'Creating a dress – evolving it – mis not just the work of days. It can stretch to weeks,' Bill Gaytten says. 'It depends on the complexity of the idea.' The working through of an idea is not done with drawings, but with patterns cut from fine cardboard which are used

59

John Galliano's own-label dress from his autumn/ winter 1995–6 prêt-à-porter show (right), worn by Kate Moss, displays the influences from his reference books, seen above and overleaf. (Photo, right: Patrice Stable Agency)

Double Georgette Dress

as templates for cutting out the shapes in muslin, called a *toile*. 'We can do as many as six *toiles* for a single dress,' he adds. 'Certainly we never get away with less than three.' Trained as an architect, he finds the process of creating garments highly stimulating. 'It's more like engineering than anything else,' he claims. 'It's finding the limits of what you can do when wrapping a body in fabric. Everything evolves. Nothing is strictly defined.'

'With John, the working tool is the *toile*. He used to give me drawings to work from but, in the end,

Overleaf: From John Galliano's own-label collection, autumn/winter 1995–67. (Photo, Mario Testino)

the *toiles* would bear no relation to them, so we don't bother now. I work on the more fantastic dresses. The most interesting part is the actual cutting. I'm excited by the ideas, the passion and fantasy of it all. John is the one who keeps pushing the barriers forward. You don't have to know how to cut in order to design brilliantly. I've never seen John cut or sew *anything*. His great skill, apart from his imagination, is in encouraging and enthusing. It's always, "Why can't we? *Why* can't we do it?" He's very hard-headed and determined

for a man who conceives such romantic dresses. We have to bash an idea around for a long time before we give up. It's usually only time that's allowed to beat us. And that is the ever-present enemy.' Even the most basic, bias-cut dress using between four and five metres of fabric will require two dressmakers to work on it for a week – and spending 150 hours on something complicated is no out of the way thing.

No one begrudges the time. The only regret is that there is not enough of it.

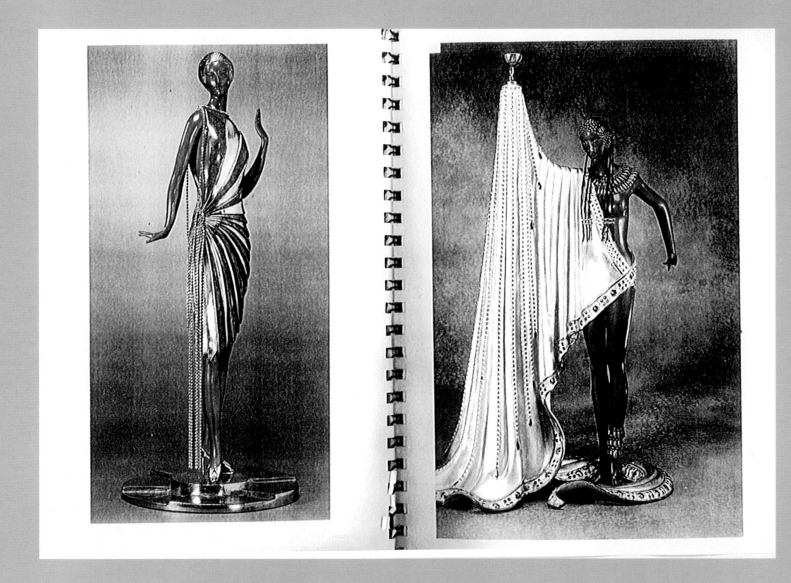

Erté's draped figures seem far removed from Galliano's bold exercise in the Nile mode as worn by actress Milla Javovich (seen here with film director Luc Besson) at the 1997 Cannes Film Festival, but the spirit, if not the material, is identical. (Photo: Bertrand Rindoff Petroff)

Behind the scenes in a couture house is a mixture of the exotic and the utilitarian as skilled hands turn a dream into practical reality. Starting with the patterns (above), and ending with the final fitting, the process involves dedication and perseverance at all stages. (Photos: Andrew McPherson)

Overleaf, photo: Lauren van der Stockt, Christian Dior archive.

'Everything is worked out. There is nothing random about a collection.'

II

LONDON:
'The Raw... and the Rarefied'

THE EIGHTIES IN LONDON dawned green, if not entirely full of the freshness of hope. It seemed as if the city were awash with young people, frequently from the provinces, determined to create their own space and articulate their own society through their dress and demeanour. They were out to question all the established beliefs and relegate most of them to the charnel house. Outrage was the message, and dress was the medium.

This was, above all, to be remembered as a period of wild images, generated by the energy and drive of the club scene, home to the 'Wannabe', when all young people felt they had the right – and the credentials – to be famous, if only for Warhol's notoriously brief span. In all the tawdriness – and there was much that was third-rate and self-deluding – there was a great buoyancy and hope. It was generated not just by belief in self, but also by the conviction that, no matter how disagreeable and hostile the real world might seem, there was the possibility of inventing a world of one's own which, in turn, would help individuals to invent themselves.

Running towards a starry future which, in the 1980s, would have seemed improbably optimistic – even to his supporters – but which the 1990s have made an undisputed fact. (Photo: Michael Woolley)

72

'When it comes to pressing, I'm the best.'

— JOHN GALLIANO

society must have had a psychological impact. Certainly, life in London dawned raw and hostile for Juan Carlos. Ready for school, he could speak no English. That was traumatic enough, but what the child found hardest to understand was the lack of vibrancy in English life. He remembered the fiestas, with their awe-inspiring emotional power; the bullfights, with their energy and drama. He looked in vain for their equivalent on the grey streets of London. And, for their loss, he found compensation.

Teenage life is difficult for many: for John Galliano it was hell. Teachers at his school found him strange and unfathomable, although not without academic ability. Some worried at his propensity for drawing costume sketches in his school books. Others scoffed. As did his fellow pupils. Beaten by teachers and bullied by boys, he felt a total misfit. 'I thought I was weird. It was only when I'd left that I realized that it was Wilson's Grammar School that was weird.'

He became an introverted, even more shy boy, and increasingly lived in a romantic dream world where, in his imagination, he could re-order history and enjoy the colour and excitement of the past. Surrounded by 'insensitive people, totally out of touch with their feminine sides', it was all that he could do in order to survive. He left school at sixteen, the earliest the law allowed, and moved to City and East London College to study design and printed textiles. It was his lifeline:

'I realized that there were other people in the world like me.'

It was from this background that he went on to St Martin's in order to complete a Foundation Year, an educational course deliberately unconstrained, in order to allow students to experience a wide range of artistic disciplines before deciding which one they would specialize in for their degree. Up to this point, John had toyed with the idea of becoming a fashion illustrator but, in fact, he decided to enrol for the BA course in fashion.

From the start, he loved it. Although he now says 'I kept myself to myself at St Martin's, creatively and socially,' he was noted by his tutors for the way he drew people to him. He was also noted for his absences, especially on Wednesday and Thursday afternoons. They knew him for a hard worker – his tutor, Sheridan Barnett, considered him a workaholic as a student – and assumed he was working at home or in a library somewhere. In fact, he was making money. Desperate to eke out the tiny funds on which he had to live, he obtained a job as a dresser at the National Theatre. And what it gave him was much more valuable and lasting than ready cash.

Working with actors like Sir Ralph Richardson and Nigel Havers on plays as diverse as *The Importance of Being Earnest*, *Major Barbara* and the latest Alan Ayckbourn, he learned to turn his hand at most things

Galliano's deep love of the theatre shows itself in his willingness to dress up and play a part for the camera. It is also a throwback to his student years when whole days were spent in creating outrageous costumes for a weekend's heavy clubbing in London's Soho. (Photo: Paolo Roversi)

No student show has
ever had the sheer bravura
of John Galliano's
'Incroyables'. Although
it lasted less than fifteen
minutes it electrified London
fashion circles with its wit,
originality and confidence.
Based on the French
revolution, it was supported
by sketchbooks showing
how clearly post-
revolutionary France had
influenced him to evolve a
completely new approach
to cutting clothes.

Right, photos: Niall
McInerney, 1984

behind the scenes. 'I was so small, I could get anywhere. In a complicated set, I could be underneath, dressing the actor. I did everything from polishing shoes to opening doors when they had to come off stage. I learned a lot, but the most important thing was pressing. When it comes to pressing, I'm the best. I was famous for it at the National. The actors would insist that they would only have their suits pressed by me.'

He was learning a skill vital to a future couturier. Balenciaga, along with Vionnet the most technically accomplished couturier of the century, believed that everything that mattered in tailoring could be achieved only by the skilful use of the iron to coax and control

fabric into behaving as it was required. John learned this basic lesson in the wardrobe of the National Theatre, a place where he was so happy that he says, 'I used to ring up the wardrobe mistress whenever I could see a space and say, "Look, things are a bit slack, can I come and do a couple of weeks for you?"'

It wasn't only to make money, it was because the theatre fired his imagination and taught him something about clothes that was not always apparent away from the heightened world of the stage: 'I used to watch Dame Judi Dench or Zoë Wannamaker in the wings, waiting to go on. I loved them both and I learned so much about a woman and her relationship with her

clothes just by watching them.' What he was observing would prove crucial in later years as he began to make theatrical demands on models, persuading them to become performers in order to show his clothes in a completely new way. He watched as the actresses, waiting for their cue, ordered their dress as an essential preliminary to commanding their space – one of the bedrocks of a successful performance.

Even as early as his second year in college, Galliano's intensity was beginning to show. He drew endlessly; he researched not only in the college library but also at the Victoria & Albert Museum; he delved into the more romantic and flamboyant periods of history. Above all, he learned everything he could about the practicalities of clothes-making. He was especially intrigued by the

cutter's skills and began to experiment with revolutionary alternatives to standard approaches. Although many of his ideas proved impractical, he had enough success to convince himself that there were other ways to cut a sleeve, or to organize a skirt to fall in a different way.

Looking back, Galliano claims, 'My fashion has been a constant evolution of ideas which I began to explore even before I had left college. I think I knew then that I had a strongly marked road to go down. All that experimental cutting led me to understand precisely how a jacket had been put together in the past; how to put it together correctly in the present and then, from that, I was led to dismantle it and reassemble it in a way that would point to the future. I never saw any

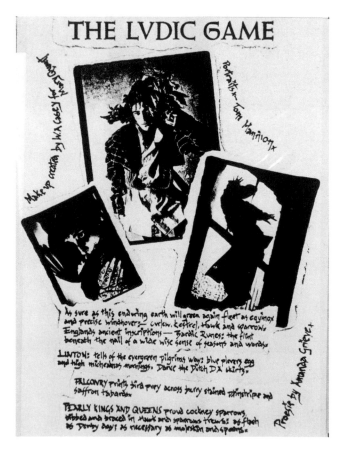

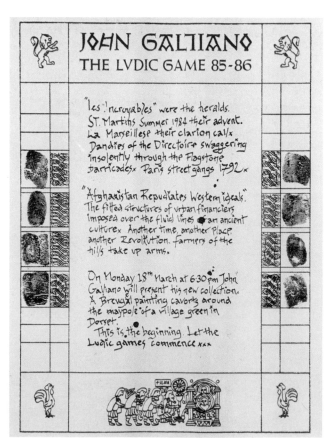

Galliano has always named his collection, often to hauntingly memorable effect. His degree show, 'Les Incroyables', was followed by 'Afghanistan Repudiates Western Ideals', in turn followed by 'The Ludic Game' and 'Forgotten Innocents': they all demonstrated the designer's radical rethinking of fashion in terms of Blake's 'Songs of Innocence and Experience': this was fashion for those previously considered too young for it.

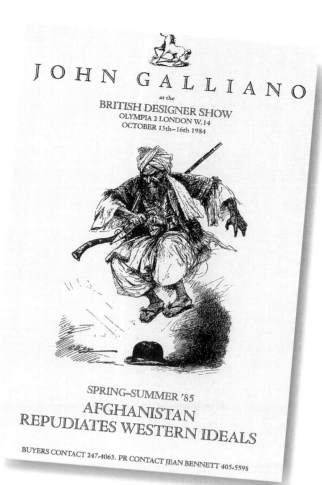

JOHN GALLIANO

at the

BRITISH DESIGNER SHOW
OLYMPIA 2 LONDON W.14
OCTOBER 13th–16th 1984

SPRING–SUMMER '85
AFGHANISTAN
REPUDIATES WESTERN IDEALS

BUYERS CONTACT 247-4063. PR CONTACT JEAN BENNETT 405-5598

point in stopping at the way in which conventional wisdom decreed a jacket should be cut. Early on, I realized how important it is just to be curious. You mustn't be frightened or hide behind pre-conceived ideas. You *have* to experiment. You just *do* it and it's beautiful because you discover an energy there which feeds you. There are no rules.'

Almost as if to prove that, John Galliano set out to discover a theme for his final year, culminating in his degree show, which would bring together the things which he had already learned – the things that mattered to him. He wanted to use the romantic beauty of the costume of the past in a way which would be not merely modern but revolutionary. He wanted to challenge the architecture of fashion – how it is cut, assembled and worn – in order to radically reform opinion on the purpose of dress. He wanted colour, illusion, drama and theatricality. He wanted what he'd

Galliano's degree show was notable for the strength and power of his menswear. It broke most of the known rules to produce a triumphantly new look. Unfortunately Galliano no longer designs for men, but many of his ideas have been taken up by others. (Photo: Paolo Roversi)

learned at the National, enjoyed in New Romanticism and been excited by in the club scene. More than anything else, he wanted to explore areas not previously examined.

He found what he was searching for in post-revolutionary France, that brief historic period which saw the flowering of fantastic fashion on the backs of disaffected, doomed youth not so very far in spirit from the young London clubbers whose numbers were soon to be cut down by the twin scourges of drug addiction and Aids. There were other similarities. Just as sexual licence and exposure of the body were characteristics of the lunatic fringe of French youth in the 1790s, so permissiveness was confused with progressiveness by their counterparts in early eighties' London. And both groups dressed the part. The New Romantics sprang from the same ideological, social and creative soil as the 'Incroyables', and their female equivalents the 'Merveilleuses', had in the brief period between the collapse of monarchist France in 1792 and the election of Napoleon as Consul for Life in 1802.

The essence of the Incroyables movement was misrule. Clothes were used as political and social weapons to show not only a contempt for civilization, but also a disregard for its standards, rules and sensibilities. Exaggeration and deformity were its trademarks. Clothes were slashed and torn; details were grotesquely enlarged; pre-revolutionary dress was parodied. Women wore high-waisted muslin dresses *à la Greque* which left little to the imagination. Men wore huge cravats, high collars and pantaloons, which were cut provocatively tightly in order to emphasize the masculine bulge.

Society was outraged, but the artists and cartoonists loved the look. It was their work which John Galliano

discovered in his researches. It was the images of the brothers Carle and Horace Vernet, affectionately capturing the more extreme fashion extravagances, that he began to copy into his notebooks. What he didn't know was that he had lighted on a group with one other similarity to the New Romantics: the Incroyables and Merveilleuses were, like all those who dress to extremes, a tiny group with a minute influence on mainstream late nineteenth-century French fashion. In the same way, New Romanticism remained largely confined to the clubs and the pages of youth-orientated style magazines such as *The Face* and *Arena*.

None of which stopped Galliano's degree show of July 1984 having an impact far beyond the confines of St Martin's School of Art. Nothing so uncompromisingly bold had previously been seen in the work of a student. Nothing had previously linked the romance and theatricality of the past so convincingly with the practicality of the present. Galliano received a first-class honours degree; a star was born and a minor period of French history, distorted and magnified by the glass of time, became part of fashion's currency. The dress designer Roland Klein was one of the outside assessors. He recalls, 'I have assessed many students over the years and, frankly, it is difficult to recall their work. I remember every piece of John Galliano's degree collection. I had never seen a student's work with so much conviction, maturity and technical skill, let alone the originality of his concepts.'

It was, as fashion folk say, a 'moment'. Galliano's clothes were the finale of the student show, the climax of a growing excitement. For days, fellow students had been helping him finish his collection. They had queued up to model it. Their exuberance and enthusiasm was entirely in keeping with the confidence and wit of the clothes. It was a benchmark show and, even before it had finished, John Galliano had, while still technically a student, become the golden hope of young British fashion, just as David Hockney had for British art in 1962 with his degree show at the Royal College of Art.

Of course, there was hype in both instances. In Galliano's case it was inevitable. The world's eyes were attuned to London fashion which was, in the words of one commentator, 'enjoying one of its frequent fifteen minutes of fame' at all levels, from club scene to salon. It already had its stars. Katharine Hamnett, David Holah and Stevie Stewart of Body Map, Stephen Linard and Vivienne Westwood were all attracting attention by outrageously breaking the rules of fashion, taste and probability. Andrew Logan's Alternative Miss World competitions delighted with their decadence. Clubs like Heaven, the Mud Club and the Beat Route were centres of the wildest new approaches, although Taboo, the best of them all, was not to open for another year. Characters like Boy George and Marilyn; Leigh Bowery and Trojan; or Scarlett Bordello with her shaved head, cupid bow lips and chicken leg earrings, and other creatures from the strange, twilight world of the sexually fluid, were always good for copy. It was a time of outrage and the world was ready for John Galliano's vision.

But not all who sat in the audience for the St Martin's Final Year Show saw Galliano's contribution merely as a continuation of the bread and circuses which London creativity had become to many media commentators. Watching carefully from her front-row seat was Joan Burstein, co-owner of Brown's, the up-

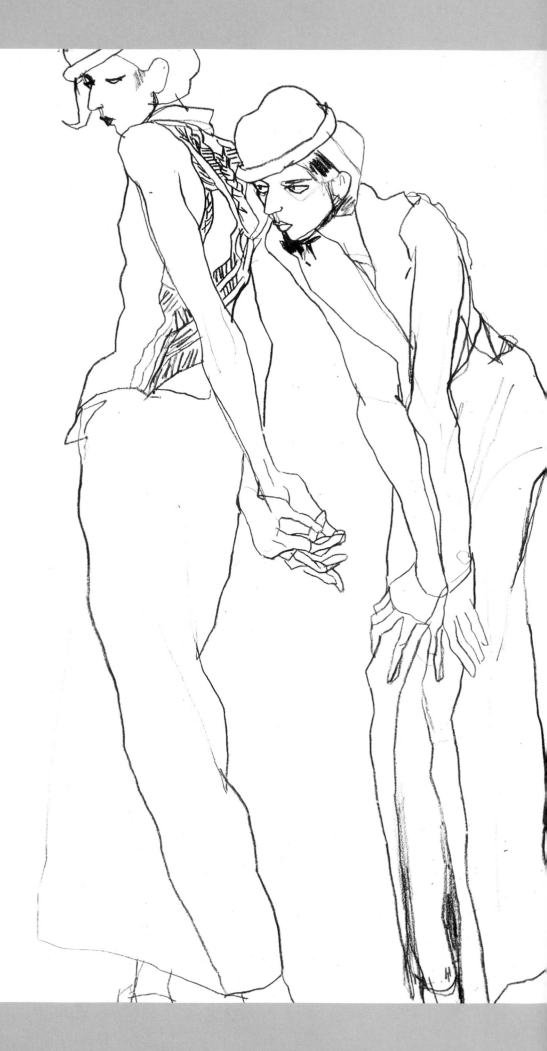

In the 1980s many fashion commentators felt that Galliano's clothes lacked the commerciality essential to sustain a career. They were wrong, as these drawings make clear: every item would be as wearable today as it was then.(Drawing by Howard Tanguy)

*Capturing the spirit of
a collection is to do
with presentation and
emphasis. How a garment is
accentuated and highlighted
enables trained eyes to
understand the underlying
fashion story of the season.
(Photo: Carrie Branovan)*

market fashion shop in South Molton Street, a woman renowned for her fashion judgement and her ability to relate to new ideas and movements which leave others baffled. Although the 'Les Incroyables' collection was composed of only eight interchangeable outfits, intended for men and women, she was amazed at Galliano's originality and verve: 'He was St Martin's best-kept secret. He was different, exciting, a free spirit.' She bought the entire collection. And, as if that were not a proof of total conviction, she went one stage further, and filled the prestigious windows of her store with it.

Neither was an act of extravagance or altruism. Joan Burstein does not take a romantic view of fashion: she is a retailer and her motives are practical. In answer to the criticism that she bought Galliano predominantly for his news value she answers, truthfully, 'We sold every piece.' As Sibylle de Saint Phalle, now head of public relations at Givenchy, but for many years one of John's closest collaborators, points out, 'Mrs Burstein was very faithful. She took the first risk. For a business woman to have the courage of her feelings to the extent that she would back a student with the conviction with which she backed John is very rare and totally admirable. She was always behind him.'

John remembers the weeks that followed as some of the most exciting of his life. 'Mrs Burstein decided on window displays when she saw the collection on the hangers, a while after the show. She invited me to do the windows and help with the selling. Initially what sold were the organdie shirts and the waistcoats. As it all coincided with my parents going on holiday, I was able to take over the house. The front room became a mini factory. There was a machine in there and we made up the clothes as the orders came through. I'd go to Notting Hill and buy old curtains and brocades; cart them home and then my friends would come in to help cut them. It was a sort of perfect cottage industry. We'd produce, deliver, get some money up front and then start the process over. Looking back, it was so amateur it had to change but, God, it was fun. Mrs B. was marvellous. She let me meet customers and did everything she could to help me reach a wider audience. It really was a very pure form of patronage and I'll never forget what she did for me.'

The buzz surrounding John Galliano in London fashion circles was growing louder, and interest in his work was spreading beyond South Molton Street. 'I remember walking past Joseph with some friends and one of them stopped at one of the windows. "Here!" she said, "They're your waistcoats. He's ripped you off!" I was quite flattered. It seemed rather special to be ripped off when you'd only just left college a few weeks but, in fact my friend was wrong. Joseph had seen them in Brown's and was so eager to have them in his shop he had bought them retail from Mrs B. And he was another one who was incredibly supportive.'

As was Amanda Grieve (now Amanda Harlech), working at that time as a stylist on *Harpers and Queen*. Like Mrs Burstein she had found John's show an explosion of imaginative ideas and radical thinking. She met him, they got on like brother and sister almost immediately and became friends and colleagues who were destined to work closely with each other for the next eleven years. She remembers the thrill of finding another person so attuned to her way of thinking that 'he finishes off your sentences for you. I loved his passion and self-belief, right from the beginning. Even then – and this really isn't hindsight – I knew he was fortune's child. I had a sense of being drawn

compulsively to John and his creativity – I knew I had to work with him.' She was styling the cover for Malcolm McLaren's LP *Fans* and she asked John to help her. Even now, he looks back and considers it one of his 'moments'. He loved working with McLaren and Amanda. They came up not with a costume, but with an enormous fan covered with strips of Chinese newspaper for a naked 'Madam Butterfly' to hide behind.

John was beginning to make contacts who would stay with him for many years, always working for little money – and often for no money at all. They didn't mind because they knew that John was even poorer than they were. He admits, 'I was a club demon. I think everybody knows by now. Music is vital to me and, in the mid-eighties, there was only one place to be. Taboo was the best.' Founded by Leigh Bowery and his friend Trojan, it so caught the frenetic mood of young London in the mid-eighties that everybody creative had to go there. Once described as an early Groucho club, but with spirit, it was much more, surpassing the Dean Street den of media folk as a place to both pose and be pretentious. As Bowery told *LAM* magazine, 'The name's a joke really. There's nothing you can't do there.'

'The club scene fed me,' John says. 'Being with other creative people like Boy George was a crucial experience to me. That's where I first met Stephen Jones, the milliner, although I'd heard of his reputation from St Martin's. Sibylle, who was later to work with me, was his assistant and so I approached him about making hats: "Please, please, will you do my show for me?"' He laughs. 'He was terribly grand, gave me that "No time for *you* sweetheart" look and that was *that*. Of course, he was doing the business then, making

There has often been a soulful beauty in John Galliano's heroines. They seem to live in a world different from the commercial and they are seen by many as beyond the reality of fashion. Their ethereal quality is enhanced by clothes which float and glide around their bodies to create a timeless romanticism. (Model, Marie-Sophie Wilson, photo:Xavier von Valhonrat)

By the late 1980s, deceptively simple shapes based on highly complex cutting techniques had become part of the Galliano design lexicon. He was a bold experimenter, pushing his techniques way beyond the line which many of his contemporaries would have feared to cross. (Photo: Galliano archives)

hats for Comme des Garçons and Montana. No time for little runts straight out of St Martin's!' In fact, Stephen Jones did eventually start to make hats for John Galliano, and it is a creative partnership which has worked extremely well. As John says, 'I love him because, apart from being so creative, he is *very* professional and businesslike – the sort of person who is passionate about every part of his job. That's what I like.'

The post Incroyables euphoria couldn't last for ever. A front room is not a sustainable base for a fashion career. Galliano needed a backer. He appeared in the form of Johan Brun (known affectionately to John and his friends as Yo-Yo), who had seen John's clothes in Brown's window. 'He was a very young entrepreneur,' John remembers. 'He said, "I want to order but I also want to manage you." We went for a few drinks together and we were clearly on the same wavelength. He asked me what I was doing and I explained the problem: "I've nowhere to work and no money to buy fabrics, but the good thing is that the shops want my clothes."' Johan found a space in a run-down building in Earl Street, just off Finsbury Park in north London. 'It was grotty but at least it was a place. We rented a small area in a studio belonging to a photographer – near the sink. So there I was, dyeing fabric, hanging it out to dry, ironing, cutting, making it up. All very *ad hoc*. Mates came in and helped where they could. It was great.' Amanda Grieve recalls it as 'a beautiful loft-like space, high up, overlooking Liverpool Street station, always full of marvellous people. Everybody came to see John there, from Boy George to Mr Francis, who made the most marvellous silk flowers in London.'

They were working towards 'Afghanistan Repudiates Western Ideals'. Not a fashion show, it was a static

display mounted as a stand, part of London Fashion Week at Olympia, and can be seen now as less a collection than a statement of intent – or even a warning shot fired across the bows of the fashion establishment. In political terms and attitude, Galliano stood as entirely his own man. He was more. His approach, radical and uncompromising, showed attitudes to dress, life and culture sharply at variance with the canons of accepted London fashion approaches. The impact of 'Afghanistan Repudiates …' rested not only with the fundamental re-thinking of the nature of dress which the pieces exemplified, but also with the fact that, beyond the overt political commentary of the title, there were layers of social and sartorial subversion.

The title, and inspiration, came from an arcane moment in history when King Amanullah Khan, who ruled Afghanistan from 1919 to 1929, issued a decree three years into his reign forbidding his subjects from wearing national costume and requiring them to dress in Western fashions. His attempts at sumptuary control, like those in Europe and America from the fourteenth to the seventeenth centuries, failed, and he was deposed. What stimulated Galliano was the idea of the people of Afghanistan trying to comply. As he told the *Daily News Record*, 'I like the idea of the tension and romance of wearing two different cultures.'

It was a collection of remarkable originality and maturity of vision for a designer who had been out of college only four months. Mixing ethnic shapes with standard British tailoring, he explained to *The Face*, 'I love the hip. My tops are baggy at the back, tight at the waist and loosing downwards after that … The idea for this collection came from a cartoon I saw in a thirties edition of *Punch* … servants and gentlemen robed in smart European dress. Just like all the Indians around the East End now ... the thing to do is to take two cultures and mix and start anew.' He did so not only with shape – the soft and the tailored – but with fabric – Indian gauze, gent's shirting and antique Empire – striped silk moiré fabrics mixed eclectically to say something new. 'It was the story of a revolt,' Galliano points out, 'so we had georgette stained with wine to imitate blood. Everything was dyed in the same bath. We used dashing oranges and maroons.' Amanda Grieve remembers discussing 'stained berry colours' with John. There were broken spectacles stuck together with sticking plaster to simulate the violence of the revolt. But it was the shapes even more than the accessories which made this small collection not only strong but exciting. As Galliano explained, 'Contours and shapes are all geared to the comfort of the body,' which meant coats with broadly accommodating sloping shoulders, and shirt sleeves sufficiently long to hang down below the wrists and function 'like gloves'. Accessories included belts with pots, pans, bells and wooden spoons dangling from them; walking sticks, pipes and glasses – all carrying labels, as if they were in a country-house auction, or even a private museum. Although the display was small, it was seminal, showing, as it did, the first signs of a thought process to which Galliano was to return frequently: the circular sleeve, the S-shaped torso and the D.A. (Duck's Arse) cut to the hem of a jacket which, Amanda Grieves maintains, he guards possessively as his own.

In an interview, John outlined his approach: 'It's all a mad mix. Everything is off balance – skirts have fronts rolled up, shirts are worn as skirts, waistcoats have rumpled fronts and halter necks – in colours such as "dried blood". I feel strongly about a way of putting pieces together,' he explained. 'I mix shapes, mix proportions. I put long over short, short over long, and break every possible rule and find different looks emerge by playing with how they are put on the body... Fashion has never been so exciting. I feel strongly for clothes wear – not men's wear nor women's wear – and it is moving right away from hard androgeny as we enter a far more dressed-up feminine mood.'

But perhaps the most prophetic comment made at this time was to *The New York Times*, when John said, 'Simple is boring... It's usually the wrong things that are more fun.' It was the attitude which was to inform 'The Ludic Game', shown on Monday, 15 March 1985, at 6.30, when, as the press handout put it, 'A Brueghel painting cavorts around the maypole of a village green in Dorset.'

John Galliano had found his Egeria, his wood nymph, his spiritual helpmate, in the form of Amanda Grieve (who later married and became Amanda Harlech), and it was her words that caught the spirit and conveyed the meaning of 'The Ludic Game'. As she wrote, 'Les Incroyables was the herald. St Martin's Summer 1984 its advent. "Le Marseillaise" its clarion call. Dandies of the Directoire swaggering insolently through the flagstone barricades. Paris Street gangs, 1792. Afghanistan repudiates Western Ideals: the fitted structures of urban financiers imposed over the fluid lines of an ancient culture. Another time, another place, another revolution. Farmers of the hills take up arms... This is the beginning. Let the Ludic Games commence.'

The *Ludi* were Roman games, secular and religious, whose purpose was to propitiate the gods and secure their protection. They followed an exact ritual and, at times, included sacrifices. Their mood was frequently

John Galliano's fashion shows have always worked on several complex levels. They are never conceived merely to show the clothes; they must convey a spirit and evoke an ideology through their styling and music as well as the choice of model. Galliano autumn/winter 1986–7. (Photos: Niall McInerney)

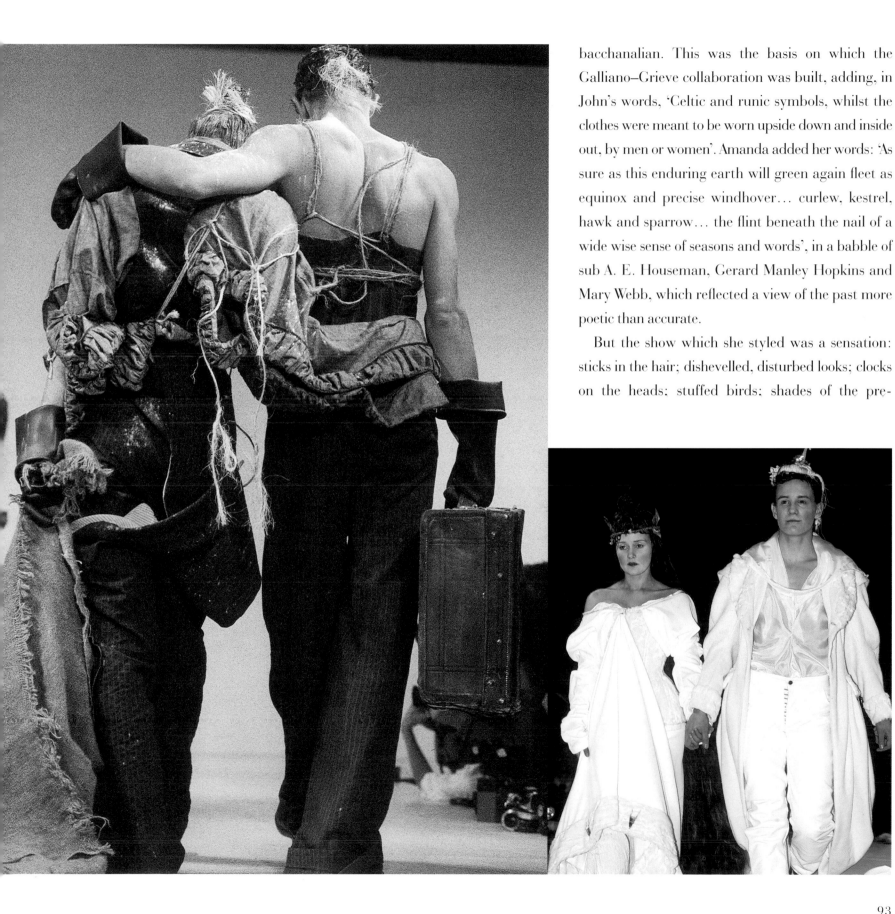

bacchanalian. This was the basis on which the Galliano–Grieve collaboration was built, adding, in John's words, 'Celtic and runic symbols, whilst the clothes were meant to be worn upside down and inside out, by men or women'. Amanda added her words: 'As sure as this enduring earth will green again fleet as equinox and precise windhover… curlew, kestrel, hawk and sparrow… the flint beneath the nail of a wide wise sense of seasons and words', in a babble of sub A. E. Houseman, Gerard Manley Hopkins and Mary Webb, which reflected a view of the past more poetic than accurate.

But the show which she styled was a sensation: sticks in the hair; dishevelled, disturbed looks; clocks on the heads; stuffed birds; shades of the pre-

Raphaelites; Ophelia; Virginia Woolf with her cardigans fastened with safety pins. It was a gallimaufry of literary allusions, Gothic statements and rural references – and it engendered mob scenes of such hysterical excitement that the British Fashion Council asked Galliano to stage a second show. Students converged on London from Manchester, Cardiff and Glasgow determined to hook into the energy of the man who many saw as a fashion messiah. The more perceptive realized that, quite apart from the brilliance of the styling and the imaginative juxtaposition of items of dress, the tailoring was as precise as that of Savile Row (where John had spent time as a student on an industrial work placement with the legendary Tommy Nutter), and the cutting as directional as anything coming from the ateliers of designers with many more years of experience.

The Ludic Game established John Galliano, making it clear that his earlier efforts were not a mere flash in the pan. Clearly, this was a talent which, for all its complexities, would survive. In fact, it was its very complexity which ensured that; since his student show Galliano has always made a strong runway statement, but it has never been simple or one-stranded. Like the man, it is multi-faceted. As Stephen Jones says, 'He's very good at keeping several images going – like juggling oranges – and, although outsiders may be in the dark, he and his team know precisely what they're aiming at, and it all works where it matters: on the runway. Because it's a small set-up, the house of Galliano is very well-organized and John is essentially hands-on. It isn't just that he has the courage to push on through the pain barrier and lose all fear. His skill is that he takes everybody with him, because he is aware of the problems with which they're wrestling.'

One of the problems, right from the beginning, was topping the last show. London fashion in the mid-eighties was a complicated cocktail of hope and hype; idealism and cynicism; volatility and predictability. As seasons passed, one of the most predictable of all developments was that young talents would be overstretched; they were all given too much too soon, and ended up burned-out and rejected. Small labels came and went as press, buyers and backers tried to come to terms with the huge explosion of fashion talent sufficiently to order it into the good, the bad and the indifferent. Although people feared for John Galliano in a field becoming increasingly dominated by commerce, no seriously informed fashion person doubted that a talent which lifted him head and shoulders above the rest would survive.

'Fallen Angels', the Spring–Summer 1986 show reinforced this opinion. To music ranging from 'Lillibullero' and 'Lord of the Dance' to rap and 'Dancing in the Streets', clouds of talcum powder thrown into the air, women's foreheads branded with the Galliano logo, hair plastered down with white mud, and items of luggage tied together with coarse string, a collection of remarkable coherence appeared. It included: Directoire dresses, ruched and gathered; marvellous shirts, high-collared and flaring; men's jackets, with huge circular-cut sleeves caught with vast buttons; fabrics layered, tucked, slashed and intertwined; and, to end it all, an array of ethereal diaphanous dresses dampened so that they clung to the body. Sibylle de Saint Phalle, one of the models, says, 'We were all characters, part of a story. John stamped his logo on our brows and, just before the finale, he threw bottles of water over us. Our clothes clung and, even more striking, the logos ran, like blood.' It was a

As the eighties drew to their end, the mixture of design purity and bold technique which were to be Galliano's most striking trademark began to show themselves in an increasingly assured line. Left: Galliano autumn/winter 1989–90; below left: Galliano spring/summer 1988. (Photos: Niall McInerney; drawing, right, Howard Tanguy)

The John Galliano logo, a modest, even amateur affair, was stamped on the forehead of the models in 'Forgotten Innocents'. For the final entrance water poured over it caused it to run in an unsettling, anarchic fashion, making the girls seem victims of some unspoken violation – an approach which was to be taken up by many designers in future years. (Photos: left, of Sybille de St Phalle, by Michael Woolley; right and far right: Niall McInerney)

classic Galliano touch, referring to the epidemic of 'Muslin Disease', that struck Paris in 1803, when women died of influenza because they immersed themselves in water before going out so that their clothes would cling to them like those in Greek sculpture. It was an ideological gesture in post-revolutionary France which had turned to the cradle of democracy in its attempts to reform society on egalitarian terms.

For Galliano, it was about purity: 'It was all to do with deconstruction. Removing the mystique and showing the reality. I piped the seams on the outside with gaffer tape.' It was also about fundamentally re-examining preconceptions – a line of investigation he took further in his next collection, 'Forgotten Innocents'. Amanda Harlech recalls it as 'a very beautiful show put

together under duress… no money… it was about seeing things as a child might. Pick up a spoon, strip away your preconceptions and it becomes a wondrous object. Forgotten Innocents was about that.' Galliano adds, 'It was about alternative ways of putting clothes together. I was experimenting with circular cutting, which causes wonderful stress to fabric, and attenuated drapes, but without tucking. I got the idea from Savile Row and how tailors cut sleeves to swing forward. We just exaggerated it by pushing it as far as it could go. It was an exercise in experimental cutting and breaking down preconceived ideas of how things could be worn – a bit like little children with a dressing-up box shovelling clothes on anyhow.'

The show opened with Sibylle, hair down to her ankles, knitting a 'cat's cradle' out of wool. Like all the

Scale, cut and volume are infinitely more important to serious designers than is pattern. As the drawings show, whether in toile (left) or finished form (right), conviction is what brings the power which makes a garment memorable. (Drawings by Howard Tanguy)

The oriental influence has been a strong and recurring leitmotif of Galliano collections over the past ten years. Clearly, the unique mixture of innocent passivity and hidden eroticism of the geisha, married to the strong theatrical appeal of formal Japanese life and manners, stimulates the designer's theatrical streak. (Photo: Xavier von Valhonrat)

models, she looked like a child. In their hair they wore 'tiaras' made of tarot cards and things found in the Thames. Although loaded with historic echoes, Forgotten Innocents was made contemporary by the juxtaposition of references: heavy with fine; rough with smooth; shapes over- and under-lapping; caught, then free – in what Amanda Harlech calls, 'The Galliano tension: purity here, rawness there; the savage and the rarefied. Its guts; its passion; its heart's blood, hot and beating, and the purity of a Communion coronet of seed pearls. It produces a creative tension, tight as a steel hawser.'

Forgotten Innocents was a watershed. It marked the end of the *ad hoc* approach. Life since college had been exciting for John, but he knew that he was living a hand-to-mouth existence that could not sustain commercial development. 'In the early days it was a question of going round the East End, buying material off the shelf from wholesalers and taking it to sweatshops where things could be made quickly and cheaply. I would cut in-house and my mum and dad would deliver the cut work to workers in south London, then bring the finished things back for me to press, ready for packing. I remember the excitement of packing the boxes – for Bergdorfs, Bloomingdales and all the top stores. We were always running out of fabric so, eventually, we decided, "This is no good. We'll have to go to Manchester and source fabric."'

But there was a more pressing need. The backing of Johan Brun had ended and, as Galliano says, 'Transferring money and getting it in on time was a problem. I only had a small account at Barclays Bank in Peckham. I was tired of sweating over stinking dye buckets and envying Body Map their glamour. I thought, "I'm virtually killing myself. Right, I want to

be professional and, even with all the help, we just can't physically do it in this set-up."' He did so through fellow designer and friend Alastair Blair, who had been set up with his own company by Danish entrepreneur, Peder Bertelsen, whose firm, Aguecheek, was backing Katharine Hamnett as well as several Italian fashion firms in London. It was known that Bertelsen was keen to fund young British talent and had even opened a shop in Brook Street, called Gallery 28, as an exclusively British showcase.

John went to see Aguecheek's business manager and, after a few preliminaries, which included John making some *toiles*, a deal was struck. *Daily News Record* of Tuesday, 1 July 1986, reporting the arrangement, pointed out that 'An Aguecheek official stressed the agreement is for one season only... the financing will be less than the £250,000 Bertelsen gave Alastair Blair.' John told the *Glasgow Herald* in May 1987, 'By the time I met Peder I was already trying to build up a discipline within myself. I knew I had to do it if my business was to survive and succeed... I haven't really changed in myself. My designs have evolved... ' and, as he was reported in *Fashion Weekly*, 'I just try to design beautiful clothes.'

The Bertelsen years gave John a much-needed stability and breathing space. For the first time since leaving St Martin's he had the security of a salary. But something was lost. Sibylle de Saint Phalle recalls the less organized, but happier, previous years. 'We all had an honest, true energy. We responded to John because he was so full of rich creative ideas. It was never about money. Nobody asked, "How much should I get?" or "What will my title be?" It was a real adventure, a team working against all odds for something they all believed in. We believed in our lives. We believed in

101

beauty. Ours was the positive energy of the young, idealistic and committed.'

John found the new situation stimulating on one level. 'It has always been part and parcel of my approach to be involved,' he says, 'in the quality, the finish, the making and the construction. I was never interested in merely being the designer. I'm passionately involved in all aspects of the business. The most exciting discoveries, the marvellous moments, aren't with the sketchbook but in the making. It wasn't all agony at Aguecheek. There were fun moments.'

There were also strong, beautifully fabricated collections which press and buyers understood. Earlier ideas were revisited and refined. Scale was reduced. The Galliano shirt – all softly controlled billows – had become a recognizable generic fashion statement. Asymetric, caught and twisted fabrics assumed a new subtlety. The trademark rose became one of many signs of high technical proficiency. The experiments continued. Understatement – of colour and line – became characteristics of the new Galliano. But it was not a fulfilling time.

'I had to start justifying myself. Previously, people had just believed in me. Now, they needed plans and projections. Everything on paper. It took time. There was lots of explaining of the ways of the rag trade. About monies, deliveries and the competition for fabrics. I knew about all these things but I constantly had to explain to the money people.' Sibylle de Saint Phalle agrees: 'Peder Bertelsen was a businessman – very successful – and he surrounded himself with businessmen rather than fashion people. And fashion is a very complex and specialist world. The Aguecheek people – with honourable exceptions – had the wrong temperament for fashion.'

In September 1987, Michael Harrison, managing director of Aguecheek, increasingly worried about rising bills and a slow growth in sales, called John in and said, 'I'm sorry, but this is crazy. Too much money is being wasted. I'm closing you down.' In fact, Bertelsen overruled the decision and John continued as part of the Aguecheek empire for another two years. He kept saying to himself, 'It's worth it: you have to have your bills paid,' but he knew that he was a horse in the wrong harness. 'It wasn't Peder,' he says. 'He understood me and was very supportive. But others were working to assumptions and formulas which I'm sure were right for them – but not for me. Our ideas were so different that even though I explained where I was going and what I was doing, and even though they listened, it all fell on deaf ears. It ended abruptly, with everything being chucked into skips.' It was the end of the decade and the end of a dream.

Paradoxically, John's name was more respected than ever. In 1988, the year when Steven Robinson, his design assistant – whom John refers to as his 'solid shoulder' – first came to Galliano on work experience from Epsom College of Art, he had been chosen as Designer of the Year for his 'Blanche Dubois' collection, and had won the Dress of the Year award at the Bath Museum of Costume. He recalls, 'After Aguecheek I sat down and said, "What do I do now?" There was no thought of stopping. The only question was how best to advance. I was tired of all the explanations and justifications. I had energy and ideas and I didn't want to waste them anymore. To use them properly I needed to work with people who understood and believed in me. Through my German agent I knew Faycal Amor. He was a Moroccan. He was aware that my mother was Spanish and this forged a bond between us. I rang him in Paris and asked for advice. It was straight from the shoulder. "Just get out. Come to Paris. Come to Paris and we'll talk."'

Galliano pleats, folds, ruches and layers the finest of materials in a complicated cocktail with an end result which has the timeless beauty of ancient Greece and the still authority of a nun's habit. (Model, Amber Valetta, photo: Galliano archive)

Overleaf: Photo: Carrie Branovan

'Curiosity: it's the most important thing.'

III

INSPIRATIONS:
Themes and Variations

D O WE CRITICIZE STOCKHAUSEN for his failure to produce tunes which might be whistled in the street? Is Willem de Kooning to be condemned because his images cannot sit comfortably on suburban walls? Are Ezra Pound's words rejected because they lack the accessibility of an advertising jingle? Trailblazers are expected to step slightly ahead of the world, opening up possibilities and formulating challenges with which we later catch up.

The same is true of fashion leaders. Their job is not to present us with clothes barely distinguishable from those currently available in the high street. Their role is to shock, stimulate, excite and amuse. Above all, they should ruffle our complacency by questioning not only our attitudes to beauty, femininity and allure, but also to ourselves.

Great painters, musicians and poets take little notice of what might please the public. They are driven by their belief that they can speak with a creative voice unlike that of anyone else. In fact, this belief in his personal uniqueness is what distinguishes the true artist from the commercial artist whose success depends on singing songs conceived by others and being paid to do so.

To interest a designer, movie stars don't merely have to be glamorous or beautiful. What is important is their personality and the strength it brings to their screen portrayals. Both Marlene Dietrich and Gloria Swanson were rich in character as well as looks – which is why they appear in Galliano's sourcebooks.

Previous page: photo by Lauren van der Stockt, Christian Dior archive.

Arrogance – of the intellectual and artistic, rather than the social kind – is the prerogative of the great designer, just as much as it is of the creators in more legitimate and acceptable creative fields. Worth set the standard in the last century. As couturier to the Empress Eugénie and the ladies of virtually every country in Europe, he knew how women should dress, and any who dared to question his judgement were instantly dismissed his salon and allowed no possibility of re-entry, regardless of power or petulance. Paul Poiret, who in the twenties was the first couturier to create a perfume bearing his name, was a total autocrat. His autobiography rings with edicts beginning, 'I decided… ', and even, 'I decreed …' Chanel, although cannily interested in making money, was content only to lead, never to follow, the women of an infinitely higher social class with whom she mixed. Balenciaga, the most austere and creatively arrogant of all twentieth-century designers, was asked to put his name to certain goods to be manufactured under licence, at huge personal profit. He refused to compromise his integrity for something as transient as money. It is this inability to compromise – not out of pig-headedness as much from sheer incomprehension of any other vision than their own – that puts certain dress designers on the level of the artist.

John Galliano joins them, for the same reason. Nobody can pretend that Galliano's career has been smooth-flowing. Though he may graze the Elysian fields now, the fashion world has been prepared to see him face ruin in the past, capable of doing little more than beating its collective breast and saying, 'Poor John. A genius – but so uncommercial.' As a judgement, it is as arrogant as it is misinformed; a knee-jerk, unthinking reaction; a blatant piece of

guilt-transference, a refusal to face the facts of the man's career.

Galliano's impact on the fashion industry, apparent even in his first show, should have been electric. It wasn't. Instead, it was ignored. Journalists became excited, retailers were interested, but the industry itself – the manufacturers, chief design executives and financiers, sitting on a moribund structure which, in real terms had hardly moved forward for a hundred years – was too lazy, complacent, and involved with making instant, easy profits to address the Galliano challenge. 'Impossible to put into production,' the pundits said, while admiring the radical new approach he was suggesting.

They were right. Galliano's cut was quite impossible to mass-produce using *existing* technical knowledge and experience. But the failure of the industry – and it failed itself as much as it failed Galliano – was to leave it at that point. Nobody was courageous and forward-thinking enough to realize the challenge and address it by finding techniques which would make it possible to manufacture such exciting clothes for a mass market perfectly ready for them. Instead of saying, 'Here is the future, we must find a way of making it possible,' a whole industry turned its back and maintained a manufacturing stasis.

The results we all know. John Galliano was the most forward-thinking and original menswear designer of the century. His clothes from the mid-eighties still look sparklingly modern, attractive and wearable – by a wide range of age groups – and yet he was forced to abandon menswear when he was backed by Aguecheek. His endless requests to include at least some men's designs in his collections were rejected as a self-indulgence. The denial was akin to cutting one of his creative veins, in a spurious blood-letting in order to make him think more 'commercially' – for which we can read 'prosaically'.

The same could be said for Galliano's female fashion. It became too easy to dub him an impractical dreamer, on his own plane, beyond help, rather than finding ways of manufacturing his clothes as he wished them to be made. He was ahead of the pack, but he wasn't that far ahead. Even now, with his name apparently secure, and his reputation as the only new designer of true stature to have emerged since Yves Saint Laurent freely acknowledged, there is still a feeling that Galliano creates clothes merely to gratify his fantasy world.

In fact, Galliano's triumph is a constant reproach to an industry too complacent to take up the challenge he has undoubtedly presented ever since his first collection. But, if the integrity of the fashion industry can be questioned, Galliano's integrity is beyond doubt. Like Chanel and Balenciaga before him, he has a handwriting unmistakably his own and undeviatingly modern. His last ready-to-wear collection, with a strong Chinese bias, demonstrated all his strengths and earned him the sobriquet of the 'Gypsy Rose Lee of Fashion' from *Women's Wear Daily* because he is 'a master of theatre, a master of fantasy. Most importantly, he's a master of making women look beautiful.'

The New York Times, reviewing his Christian Dior ready-to-wear collection, took the opportunity to add its accolade: 'Despite pale imitations that keep springing up, no one could mistake Mr Galliano's design for that of another hand. At Christian Dior, much of the wrenching beauty of Mr Galliano's clothes was in the dramatic styling that his team has perfected

beyond compare… with an unmatched understanding of what makes women romantically sexy and beautiful.' Such encomiums are not lightly given but, for Galliano, they are not new. The disgrace of the fashion industry is that John Galliano has been rated extravagantly high since the beginning and yet his challenge was seen as too great to be taken up at manufacturing level.

Many will say that the practicality of John Galliano's work is its least important feature. Certainly, it is a point of view worthy of contemplation. But John Galliano would reject it. For him, a show, vital as it is, is a figurehead for a ship which is entirely commercial. He would claim that, without its ship, a show – no matter how magnificent – becomes an empty thing, a façade, a meaningless piece of decorative trivia, rather like the figureheads from old sailing ships found in cleaned-up, sanitized, theme-park ports and harbours. Galliano's ship currently consists of ten collections, eight of them for Dior. The clothes shown to the press in ready-to-wear and couture are less than a quarter of the total output. It is because three-quarters of his designs are primarily for production that talk of his uncommercial and impractical approach irritates him.

Galliano tells a story from his early days, concerning his fabrication. Tired of trying to buy fabric from London wholesalers, he decided to go to the north of England to source his own fabric supplies. 'We went all over Yorkshire, visiting mills where they had marvellous unwashed wools with no silicone finishes. Although I had no money, I was excited by experimental fabrics, even then. One I'll never forget was called Linton tweed. It was green and black with a mohair overcheck. It looked as if a sheep had caught its fleece on barbed wire. I loved using it.' The same practical

'He adores women. That's why he always needs the close presence of a woman in his intimate team.'

— MANOLO BLAHNIK

and directly confrontational approach to production has been the unknown but vital other side to the glitteringly extravagant Galliano coin throughout his career.

Just as the great artists of the past ground their own pigments and prepared their own surfaces before allowing their brushes to be carried away by their imaginations, so a great couturier must have a balance between his creative and practical side, if he is to survive. Fantasy which is not realizable is as sterile as practicality with no imagination. All of the great couturiers have been technicians — although only Chanel and Balenciaga could cut and sew as well as the top hands in their ateliers — as much as they have been artists. Indeed, there are many fashion commentators who insist that creating clothes is much more a craft than an art.

They are wrong, while appearing to be right. At any one time, the number of supreme exponents is small; the number of the competent but inspired is considerable. For one Chanel, there were hundreds of dressmakers in Paris who stood out above the thousands more that clustered there in obscurity in the thirties. Who but the most arcane specialist now recalls Bruyère, Lafaurie, Nicole Groult or Agnès-Drécoll, all of whom kept quite sizeable and very chic Parisian

establishments and were regularly featured in *Vogue*, *L'Officiel*, *Femina* and *Le Jardin des Modes*? And does it matter that their names are lost? Chanel and others of the time, such as Schiaparelli and Molyneux, give validity to what the rest were achieving, but they alone rose above the crowd and, in their rising, put fashion on a different plane.

Still today, in the hands of the majority of practitioners fashion struggles to be accepted as even a minor art. It exists in a strange, twilit landscape, a staging post between high art and high camp, with a little of this, a little of that and lot of what the fashion world itself calls 'rock and roll' — a mixture part-Disneyland, part-Hollywood B-movie, with more than a dash of emotional self-indulgence. It's a world which those outside find hard to take seriously; a world which often has difficulty in separating the meretricious from the worthwhile; a world where the romance of the fight against justice attracts people to the theatricality of Byron more readily than the pragmatism of Garibaldi; a world of taste which prefers its décor designed at second hand by Nancy Cunard or Elsie de Wolfe rather than the Adam brothers or Chippendale.

But it is a world which occasionally throws up people who transcend its tawdriness, people who remind us that good fashion is like good art —

The sophistication of perfect purity of line has always been understood by Galliano. Like Captain Molyneux — a British designer who also moved to Paris to make his name, and who became an icon for Christian Dior — Galliano constantly returns to this concept of 1930s understatement, as he did with this bias-cut dress for his 1994 collection. (Photo: Paolo Roversi)

dangerous, challenging and frightening. People like John Galliano, secure in their position *vis-à-vis* the past and the future.

In his debut couture show for Dior, Galliano deliberately echoed some of the lines and fabrics which had made the original Dior griffe so strong. He had been attracted to Dior's spirit even before his appointment to the house. His Galliano ready-to-wear show in October 1994 in the Pin-Up photographic studio in Paris had contained dresses in the Dior spirit, as had his Givenchy shows. Certain fashion journalists, aware of how rife it is in the industry, whispered plagiarism. They failed to understand the difference between the second-rate copy of the uninspired, and the transposition of a vision by a man as gifted as the original creator.

In fine art, it is a distinction well understood. Would anyone condemn Picasso as a plagiarist in his reworkings of Velázquez? Would Van Gogh be criticized for the way he used the genius of Delacroix to create something that echoes the original but is uniquely his own and, as such, truly original? John Galliano's gleanings spring from the same spirit.

The roots of Galliano's intellectual and creative response are not easy to expose. He surrounds himself with a close-knit team with which he works so intimately it is difficult to uncover the well-springs of his imagination. Like many creators tired of unanswerable questions — or questions not worth the answering — he plays with journalists. For example, to one he claims never to have read a book; then to another boasts that he has read the whole of Proust. Both claims are clearly untrue. John Galliano is the sort of artist who absorbs stimuli rather than searching for them intellectually. He has had considerable help. His

musical knowledge has been broadened by his association with Jeremy Healy so that he can claim, 'I'm not afraid of "big" music. I love opera as well as Michael Jackson or Madonna. Currently I'm listening to Bach and Chopin before I come into work in the morning.' Everybody close to him knows how important it is for John to work to a musical background. At Galliano, if they want to find him, they just follow the sound.

But it is painting which has the greatest and most immediate influence on fashion designers. They all have a favourite period: for Vivienne Westwood it is the sixteenth and seventeenth centuries; for John Galliano, it is the golden period of wealth and privilege from the Belle Epoque to the outbreak of the First World War. He adores the portraits of Giovanni Boldini, Italy's master of 'flash and scintle' portraiture whose work, although artistically second-rate, captures the fashion of his time — not only in the clothes that were worn, but in the *way* that they were worn — better than many artists intellectually and technically his superior. He is the undisputed chronicler of the belle époque. Gertrude Stein was so enthusiastic about Boldini that she predicted that he would eventually 'be recognized as the greatest painter of the last century'. Bernard Berenson was more circumspect, although he also considered that Boldini 'perfectly captured the female elegance of the era', adding, 'the compelling enchantment of his portraits reveal not only the sure, impulsive qualities of the painter, but also a certain satirical bite'.

Boldini is one of a triumvirate of artists working in the last decades of the nineteenth and first years of the twentieth centuries whose fashionable portraits have inspired John Galliano. The Americans John Singer

Sargent and James McNeill Whistler both painted portraits which, like those of Boldini, captured the fashion mood of the moment. Like Tissot, they were all in love with elegance and set out to convey the vibrancy and spirit of their sitters through an interpretation of their highly fashionable dress.

It was Boldini's dashing brushwork which produced the most dazzling results. His portraits of Mrs Howard-Johnstone, the Countess Zichy and the Duchess of Marlborough all epitomize not only the period's high-fashion dress, but also the Edwardian glamour stance, with the body provocatively twisted into a pouting shape. And it is, of course, the same line as Galliano's famous 'S' shape. But it is the portrait of the Marchesa Casati which has most influenced the designer – not merely for its brilliant handling of paint and stylish palette limited to black and purple, but also for the legend that surrounds the name of the sitter.

The Marchesa Casati is the perfect fashion icon. Rich, glamorous and wilful, her private life and public appearances vied with each other over which could create the most scandal. Her appearance was memorable; her lifestyle enviable. D'Annunzio confessed, 'She was the only woman who ever astonished me.' She went through many fortunes and, by 1932, had amassed debts of over $20 million in modern terms.

Her extravagance was exemplary, as were her parties. She adored fancy dress and had Bakst create costumes for her, although her appearance was sufficiently arresting even in normal dress. Her face was always chalk white, her hair was dyed a brilliant orange – in defiance of all the canons of lady-like behaviour at the time – and her eyes were rimmed heavily with black kohl and, frequently, given extra

impact by being outlined with black tape. The décor of her homes was extraordinary, but what made them legendary was the wild creatures the Marchesa kept as pets, including monkeys, snakes and a leopard.

Couturiers adore such exotics, their lives and attitudes feeding their imaginations as much as their dress and appearance. What appeals to John Galliano in such women is an extravagance of emotion, taste, style and gesture in defiance of a more mundane world. Not that inspiration comes only from the rich playing out an outrageously self-indulgent life against a background of wealth and privilege. Strength of character, the ability to control life and live it as one pleases, outside the norms of social behaviour, are the attraction, regardless of wealth or status.

That is why he takes a woman like Man Ray's mistress Kiki of Montparnasse as an inspiration with as much enthusiasm as he does any fabled aristocrat. Kiki came from humble origins and, at the age of thirteen, was apprenticed to a baker. Blackening her eyebrows with matchsticks to make her look older, she ran away and became an artist's model – a contemporary euphemism for mistress – at the age of fourteen. Tempestuous, wildly wilful, she felt totally at home in the twilight world of the Parisian *demi-monde*, mixing with pimps, cocaine pushers, drunks, drug addicts, down-and-outs and impecunious painters.

She became Chaim Soutine's model and mistress and was passed from him to various other artists before ending up with Man Ray, who photographed her many times. Her sexual appetite and willingness made her a legend, as did her filthy songs and outrageously aggressive behaviour in the cafés of Montparnasse. She thought nothing of appearing naked, and frequently performed obscene feather dances on table tops. Her heavy figure had more in common with one of Picasso's monumental females than the delicacy of the Marchesa Casati, but her face had a spiritual quality as well as a peasant directness. It appealed to Ernest Hemingway, who admired her make-up – strongly outlined eyes and deep red cupid's bow mouth – sufficiently to write, 'Having a fine face to start with, she made it a work of art.'

Another woman who inspired artists and writers of the period was Chanel's friend and rival, Misia Sert. She was a heroine after John Galliano's own heart, which is why he called one of his fashion presentations 'Misia Diva'. Thrice married, patron of the arts, she was an enchantress even as a child. Her vitality and skill at playing the piano enraptured Liszt and Fauré. She became friend and muse to Diaghilev and, through him, inspiration for Nijinsky, Bakst and Stravinsky. She was painted many times by Toulouse-Lautrec, Renoir, Bonnard and Vuillard. Proust described her as both a marvellous creature and 'an historic monument'. She was the inspiration for two characters in *The Remembrance of Things Past* – Princess Yourbeletieff, whom he described as a 'most priceless treasure', and Mme Vendurin, a woman who pushed her way to the top of Parisian society, rather as Misia herself did. For the musician Erik Satie, she was a 'magician' and, for Cocteau, 'beauty of soul was so natural to her that no one noticed she had it'. When she died, half-blind and addicted to drugs, in 1950, Chanel laid her out, dressing her in white against a bank of white flowers, a pale pink satin ribbon and a single pink rose on her breast. She was mourned as the most significant of all the artistic muses of twentieth-century art.

For a man with John Galliano's sensibility, women of the past have a greater allure than heroines of the

The famous turn-of-the-century fashion icon, the Marchesa Casati, believed in emphasizing her eyes with heavy applications of kohl. For John Galliano's autumn/winter 1995–6 collection Stéphane Marais created a soft and flattering make-up based on the Marchesa's principles. (Photo: Jean Marc-Manson)

present. Rita de Acosta Lydig, always known as 'the fabulous Mrs Lydig', spent a fortune on dress and was especially obsessed with shoes. She had them made for her out of medieval velvets and lace by Yanturni, a curator of the Cluny Museum, who demanded a deposit of $1,000 before he would begin, and often kept her waiting for years before he delivered them. Her shoe-trees were made from old violins and her shoes travelled everywhere with her in a trunk made of Russian leather, lined with satin. Gaby Deslys, more soubrette than actress, more grande cocotte than either; the famous courtesan Liane de Pougy; Marie Lani, the German actress painted by Matisse, Dufy, Derain and Vlaminck, among others: these are the kind of women who spend the first halves of their lives hung with sapphires and diamonds and draped in sables and chinchilla, then, as their beauty fades, they face an existence of empty rejection.

They are the women who inspire a romantic like John Galliano, even though he isn't always aware of their names. Their's are the faces that appear and re-appear in his sourcebooks, sometimes named, more often not, as the personification of the face, the style, the image for which he is subconsciously searching. They are the outsiders as well as the catalysts for society; their lives are a labyrinth of ups and downs; their end is almost always lonely. Romanticism is frequently tinged with pessimism; there is no escaping the feeling of doom at the end of the charade and this is the quality which distinguishes John Galliano's heroines.

Even as early as 1986, with his Fallen Angel and Forgotten Innocent collections, Galliano's women had an element of the victim. They were delicate, fey things, alluring because they were so vulnerable. His present-day heroines have seen more of the world; they've kicked around a bit; they appear to be in charge of their sexuality and their lives but, underneath it all, they are the victims his women have always been. It is no accident that, alongside his glorification of the exotic in the form of real-life characters such as the South American thirties actress Dolores del Rio, he keeps returning to fictional characters who could easily have stepped from the pages of Chekhov or Tolstoy, or the plays of Tennessee Williams, heroines such as Blanche Dubois, from *A Streetcar Named Desire*, with her broken life and desperate yearnings, whom the theatre critic Kenneth Tynan described as 'worldly-weak' but 'pure in heart and vision'.

He could have been describing the Modigliani woman whose face has such a power over John Galliano. Dark Mediterranean eyes, a certain mouth, set in a blandly oval face – the attraction seems a very personal and private thing. Perhaps it links with early memories of his mother, whose Spanish qualities have had such an effect on him – an effect which combines the gaiety and sobriety, the dream and the doom of the Spanish mentality in a heroine hopeful and fearful at one and the same time.

The other significant characteristic of a Galliano heroine is the fact that she is always escaping, searching for a different and better life, away from Russia, out of school, or beyond the confines of a gypsy encampment. And her escape invariably involves exploitation of her sexuality. In this respect, Galliano appears to have changed over the years. His early heroines had a delicate, accidental sexuality. Like early rosebuds, their attraction lay in their fragility and vulnerability. Now, his female image is projected with a raw and raunchy libidinous confidence which pulsates beneath the surface of the clothes, bringing echoes of hookers, geishas, hostesses in opium dens and even transvestites. John, we are told, loves women, but it is not easy to avoid the thought that, within that love lurks a fear which must be laid to rest by pastiche or, even more compelling, the suspicion that it is a love so intense that it also encompasses a degree of hatred.

Spirit and flesh – and their apparent incompatibility – are major well-springs of dramatic tension and it is surely not fortuitous that the tension is increasingly apparent in Galliano's shows as he strides towards his maturity as a creator. After all, the theatre gave him his first 'hands-on' experience. It is surely to be expected that such a liberating opportunity in his formative

CLOSE-UP: Creating the Show

ALTHOUGH THEY ARE PROBABLY the most sought-after invitations in the entire fashion world, not all fashion writers and buyers are convinced of the validity of John Galliano's unique and idiosyncratic way of styling his clothes for their first presentation to the world. Those who see clothes as entirely practical artefacts of modern life are uneasy about what they judge to be a wilfully whimsical approach – and their unease begins with the invitation.

Invitations to John Galliano fashion shows are unlike any others. Carefully judged to capture both the mood of the clothes and their presentation, they give much more information than mere venue and time. Essentially, they are the first romantic contact between couturier and audience: an invitation to suspend disbelief and to enter Galliano's world on Galliano's terms. Above all, they are a declaration of intent.

An invitation to a Galliano fashion show is no pedestrian thing. As much effort goes into it as any other aspect of a presentation because he knows that this is his opportunity to convey the spirit which captures the imagination even before the first dress has appeared. (Photo: Andrew McPherson)

120

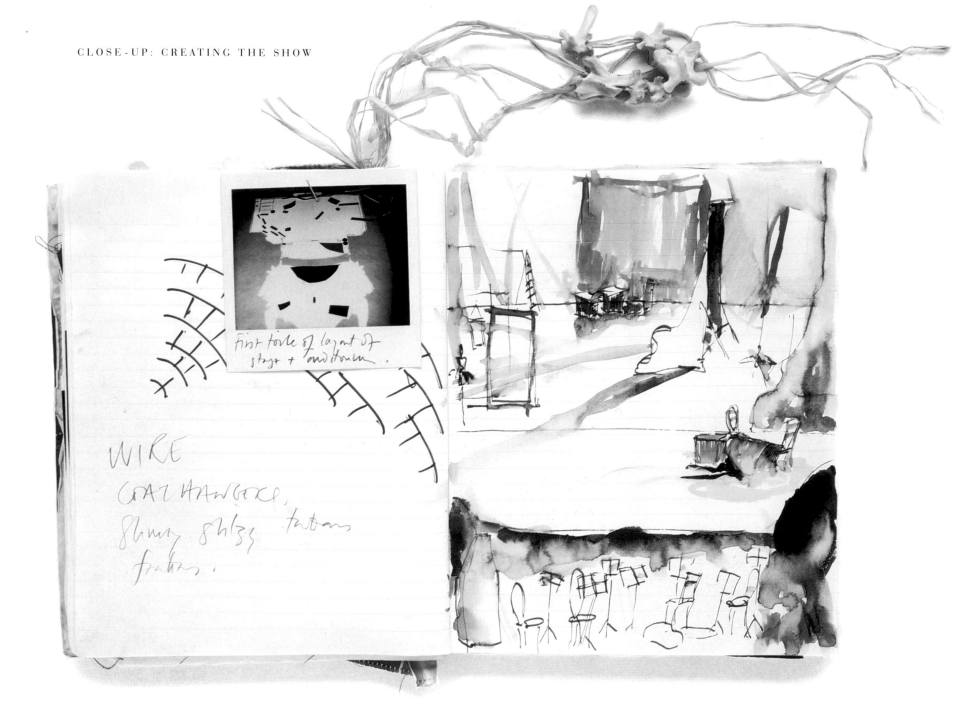

An amateur boxing promotional hand-out from the twenties; a Russian doll containing a silver charm bracelet; some desert sand, a bullet and a cache of love letters; a ruby-red ballet slipper and a rose; a hastily written telegram, a rusty key with a handwritten label; even a fifties style school report – such things can infuriate as much as delight. But nobody throws these invitations away, no matter how much they may be irritated by what they see as a fey refusal to come to terms with the real world. And the reason they don't is simple: love it, or hate it, a John Galliano show – either for his own name collection or for Christian Dior – is an unmissable experience.

It is also challengingly different from any other shows, and takes weeks of involvement from John and his team, who see it as a much more positive and creative thing than merely the vehicle for showing clothes. To them, it is integral to the whole concept of the clothes, in the way that a Renaissance frame is to a picture or a jeweller's setting is for a gem: the one loses something without the other. John Galliano would go further and say the one is seriously weakened without the other. In his mind, the clothes and their presentation are indivisible.

For those who haven't witnessed a Galliano presentation, it is important to know what it is – and

Creating the mood of a John Galliano show depends on conjuring the right atmosphere in the venue. Much work and planning goes into the mise en scène, whether it is in order to create a peasant circus, the downtown area of an American city in the fifties or a Hollywood film set in the thirties.

122

is not. To begin with, it is meant to be an intimate, interactive occasion for a severely limited number of guests. Most French shows expect to seat well over a thousand people with many guests standing; a Galliano own-name show is limited to 500-odd seats with, officially at least, no guests standing. Traditional runway shows have banks of seating ranged on either side of the raised runway, placing press on one side and buyers on the other. The prime position, reserved for the top journalists, VIPs and photographers, who stand behind them, is at the end of the runway. The seating is hierarchical and divisive. Depending on the designer, and how he and his press and PR staff rate individuals, publications, stores and manufacturers, everyone is seated according to status, power, buying and publicity clout and, although most are happy with their placing, there are inevitably mistakes ending in ruffled *amour propre*.

Galliano's approach avoids such pitfalls. Eschewing the angular, raised runway as being too constraining, he chooses venues which allow his models to stroll a serpentine line through several rooms. Whereas in a traditional show the climactic moments are when the models reach the end of the runway, in a Galliano presentation there are many different moments. As his press officer, Mesh Chhibber explains, 'John feels that

123

it is very important to create a sympathetic atmosphere. He insists that as many guests as possible should have a good view. We have as many front row seats as possible by lengthening the distance, stringing it out through several rooms. He also breaks down the audience barriers. He won't have press all blocked together in one place, and buyers in another. He mixes them, and the nationalities. The only thing he insists upon is practical: writers for newspapers must have good seats because, unlike the rest of the audience, they usually have to turn around their copy immediately. They don't have time to come to the showroom and

examine the clothes, so they must have an uninterrupted view that enables them to see everything at the show.'

Mesh maintains that the Galliano system makes his life easier because there is no one prestigious room in which all the guests feel they have a right to be. All rooms through which the models pass have their own *mise en scène* with their moments of drama and excitement worked out and created by John and the team. When they have decided where the key point of each room is to be, the photographers are placed accordingly. They are crucial to how the room is to be

Amanda Harlech was for many years involved with creating the atmosphere of a show with John Galliano. Her notebooks are a vivid chronicle of two minds steadfastly following one creative path, crammed as they are with notes, sketches, polaroids and swatches of material.

bunch of roses...

The Aid Ballet shoes awaiting dispatch.

'worked' because they give the models a focal point to which they can act. As John says, 'There is nothing random about the show. It is all carefully planned, like a film. And the venue and how it is to be is decided early on – in tandem with the clothes, really. In other words, as we are designing the clothes, we are thinking not only how they will work together but also how they will work within the story. How they will help to *tell* the story.'

As with a film set, the dressing of the venue is vitally important. The set designer with whom John prefers to work is Jean-Luc Ardouin, who might be asked to create a rooftop scene, a gypsy circus, or even, as he did for the Galliano Autumn–Winter 1997 collection, shown in the Musée Nationale des Monuments Français in the Palais de Chaillot in March 1997, a Cecil B. de Mille-style film set. The props required are always considerable, but for the 'Suzy Sphinx' show, as it was known, the demands were formidable. Suzy, the heroine, was taken from an English girl's school, through Egypt to Hollywood, where she ended up playing Cleopatra in a film. A story-line rich with ironies required a setting with the same mood. The props not only had to be authentic, they also required a camp quality that would send up the kitsch atmosphere of Hollywood B-movies without allowing the humour to undermine the magnificence. So, along with peacock thrones, obelisks, fallen Egyptian masonry inscribed with hieroglyphics, sand, rich fabrics, pottery and copper, there was film lighting, camera bogies and their railway tracks, all skillfully mixed to stimulate the audience imagination and make it receptive to the overall tale even before a model appeared.

In order to create such elaborate sets, it is not merely money and hard graft that are required. The venue, once chosen, must be passed as safe with both the fire and security authorities. 'The *préfecture* of police liaise with us through the show specialists,' Mesh says. 'The regulations about numbers and safety are much more stringent in Paris than in London. For example, no one is allowed to be more than fifty yards from a fire exit, which clearly dictates the décor and how each room and its seating may be laid out.' Steven Robinson adds, 'Dressing a set is a long process of trial and error. It can take weeks to find the perfect Empire chair. When Amanda was a part of the team she used to take on a lot of the responsibility, because she always knew how to interpret what John wanted it to be.' John agrees. 'She was marvellous at making things look as if they'd just casually come together, almost by accident, but it takes an incredible amount of time and determination to get everything right.'

The set takes three days to assemble and dress, and John checks everything, working as a stage director. Every night – sometimes it is well past midnight if fittings have been complicated and time-consuming – he goes to the venue – where everyone is still working – to check that the day's work has fulfilled his brief. Invariably, there are adjustments to be made: 'That lighting is too bright' – Galliano uses theatrical rather than runway lighting – or 'That yellow is too strong' – clearly, all colours are chosen to complement the fabric

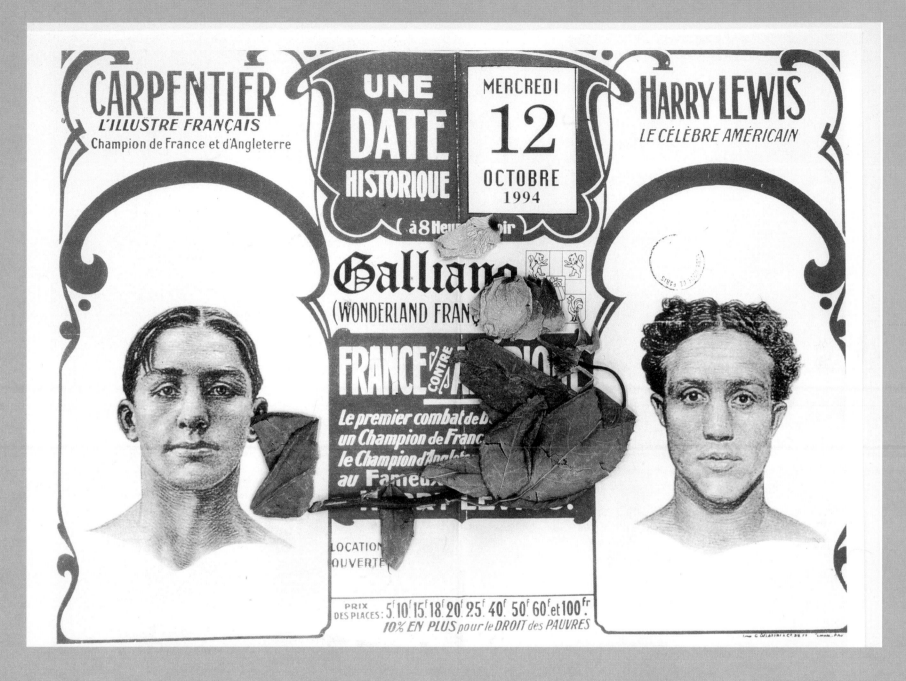

School reports, boxing promotional hand-outs, Russian boxes and (overleaf) telegrams, desert sand and bullets have all been used as invitations to Galliano shows. For true fashion followers, they are collector's items from the moment they are received.

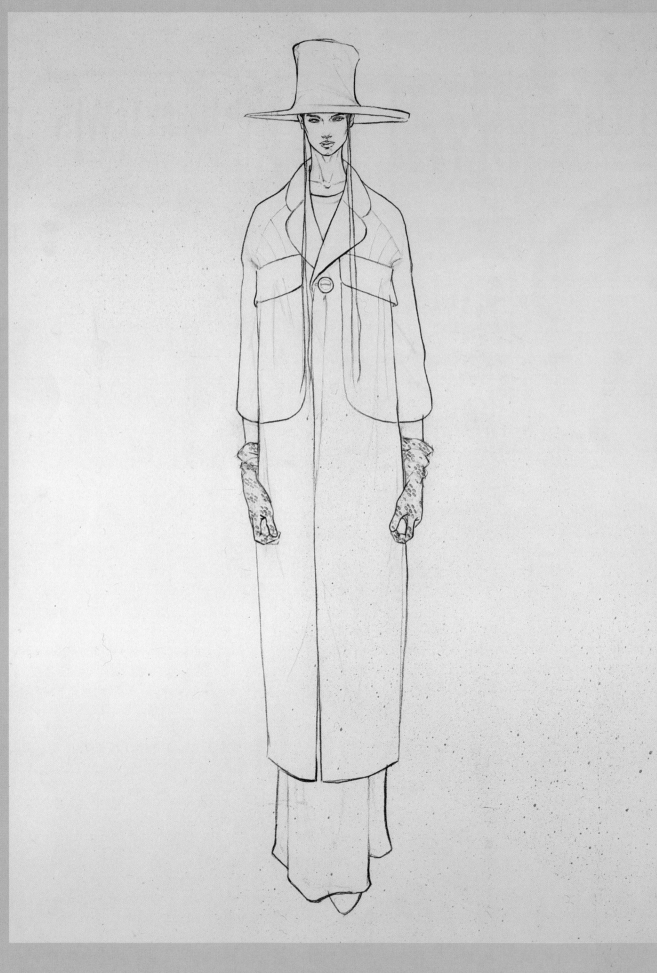

It is forgotten that John Galliano's clothes in the 1980s had a strong linear quality and a bold sense of scale. The result of a highly developed and precise fashion sense, they were the qualities which raised his work above that of all the other fashion wunderkind jostling for attention in London at the time. (Drawing Claire Smalley)

of the clothes. It is the culmination of at least a month's involvement from John and his team, looking at Polaroids, making colour tests, checking fabric swatches and approving artefacts that will dress the set. As with the dresses, the music, and every other aspect of the show, nothing about the venue is left to chance. It is rightly seen as the vital setting for that once-only opportunity to sell the Galliano story, in all its ramifications, for the coming season.

There are others outside the house whose role in the selling process is crucial: the make-up and hair specialists; the shoemaker and the milliner. Stephen Jones has created hats for Galliano shows since John moved to Paris, including his Givenchy and Dior collections. Although the hats are produced especially for the show and do not go into production, they are seen as a vital part of the Galliano projection. As Stephen Jones says, 'A hat can kill an outfit completely – or it can make it. John takes hats very seriously. He sees them as integral to his clothing statement. He dresses the woman in his head and the hat requires as much effort as any other part of the collection.'

He has his first discussions about five weeks before the show. 'John talks me through the collection. It's a wonderful performance. He explains very carefully what the collection is about – the themes, the places, the time, and masses of widely different references. The initial briefing can stretch to four or five hours of talk. At that point, John has the outfits numbered on blank pieces of white paper, but nothing drawn. There will be sourcebooks everywhere and maybe one or two preliminary sketches of a jacket shape or a silhouette. I take notes, but they're not important. What matters is catching the spirit, although I don't always come away with a strong idea of where the collection is likely to go.'

Stephen will produce between forty and fifty sketches, and he normally starts work immediately, sketching on the journey back from Paris to London. 'The spirit is a fragile thing,' he says. 'I like to catch it immediately. If I don't, it will go. five days after our meeting, I start faxing my suggestions and if I feel very sure about how the collection will evolve I might go straight into *toile* in my workroom. Many people have difficulty in reading a sketch and, although John *can* understand sketches, he would never make a decision until he had seen a 3-D object. "Yes," he says, "I like the idea, but…" The faxed drawings are nothing more than working documents with notes about scale, colour and trimmings.'

It is when John and his team see the *toiles* that things begin to move. 'I do a presentation of my own,' Stephen continues. 'Sketches, toiles, and *my* sourcebooks, which are not necessarily about hats, but contain elements that can inspire shapes and details. By this time the collection will have advanced. The thinking could have moved forward, so that what we're looking for is not necessarily what we originally discussed. The field has begun to narrow and John is in a position to say how many day, cocktail and evening outfits there will be. I'm always terribly nervous when I present because if I get it wrong and John doesn't particularly like anything, it's awful because he's so polite. I'm saying, "Tell me!" and, of course, he can't because he doesn't

The milliner Stephen Jones has collaborated with Galliano for many years, producing a series of 'ideas' sketches as well as finished drawings, toiles of the hats and, finally, the objects themselves – always perfectly judged to complement the clothes as well as highlight the unique look of each of the models.

know at that point. But one of his great strengths is that he keeps his mind entirely open. We try the hats on one of the women, working on it in front of a mirror and, as we move it around, I watch John's expression. All the time, I'm thinking, "What is it he likes – the hat, how it interacts with the hair and forehead, or the colour?" It's a process of divining whether it is the hat or the angle which he likes – the line of beauty. What I like about millinery – and I know John shares this view – is that it is much more about beauty than about fashion.'

It is at *toile* stage that John and Stephen begin to discuss hair. By now, the numbered sheets are blank no more. The sketches on them already have a consistent, if rudimentary, hairstyle. As Stephen says, 'It is vital for the hat not just to sit there, but to become an organic part of the head, which includes hair and make-up. It's a recipe that changes for each girl according to her personality and the character of the dress. When John is looking at a hat he is subconsciously pencilling in a hair-do to go with it.'

Ten days before the show, Stephen moves to Paris so that he can be part of the increasingly fast-paced creative process. 'I have to be there to react, to keep up, to know the changes which take place and to supervise

Many hours of hard work are required to create a hat of couture standard. No corners are cut or expense spared in the search for the perfect line of beauty which all good millinery must have. (Above, Givenchy prêt-à-porter, spring/summer 1997, designed by John Galliano photo: Anne Deniau, Givenchy archives; right: Christian Dior haute couture, spring/summer 1997, photo: Lauren van der Stockt)

the making of the hats to John's specifications. I personally work on the hats at this stage – although there are others there to do the five miles of slip-stitching! John wants the hats to be gorgeous things, just as everything else in the collection is. He wants me to find the perfect petersham band for inside, the perfect silk satin lining. He expects me to do these things properly, although they can't happen quickly. He sees hats, shoes and handbags as objects in their own right – precious, beautiful things worth taking time and trouble over. To work with a designer who values and understands things like that – who demands them although they are very expensive – enriches the whole experience. It's a counsel of perfection. Even things that can't be seen must be done as perfectly as possible. To work on that level of finish is the reward for the countless nights spent working through, for Air France being three hours late …

'Hats must be expressive – lighthearted, humorous, glamourous – they must articulate the couturier's feelings. John and I view hats in the same way. He wants from a hat what I want. He knows that a hat can

lift the whole outfit. John's attention to detail is for nobody but himself. He wishes to please nobody. He wishes only to do it right. John is a designer who knows hats – lots don't – and if he says no, I go with that because I respect what he brings to his judgement. We reduce the forty-fifty sketches down to about twenty *toiles*. Most outfits have some form of headgear. We throw out and add more – then we put in the final things. We won't use them all. Once made up, some won't work; others are redundant because the outfits have changed. Seven out of eight of the hats are used. The rejection comes from reasons not necessarily to do with the hats.

'My job at this stage is to give the hat its life. I can come in, slice it up and make it into something John hasn't asked for but which I know he wants. I can be objective and even ruthless. I'm always ready to change a hat to give it that zing. I always fit it on the girl herself and I talk to her, listen to what she says and often change the angle or whatever in the light of what she's said. And I brief the model as I put it on. She poses and I decided with her what way she should wear it, how she should move. As I say, "This is the way your hat is. Now, you make it your own."'

John Galliano's shoemaker is Manolo Blahnik, far and away the most inventive, witty and iconoclastic *bottier* working today. But what makes him so successful is that his shoes are not only glamorous, they are also feminine; they are light-as-air but essentially practical. It is for these reasons that he and John work together so well. Manolo responds to what he describes as the rigid creative self-control that he finds in Galliano. 'He hides it under that nonchalant English attitude,' he claims. 'But it is there – the ruthless pursuit of excellence. He has learned the importance

of discipline. He has exquisite refinement and a wonderfully fine eye, but what is marvellous about him is his ability to trigger ideas and begin thought processes. It's amazing how focused and efficient he has become since moving to Dior. Very to the point.'

Blahnik's role does not require the same close involvement as Stephen Jones's does. In fact, he and John understand each other sufficiently for the shoe story to evolve from only one meeting and a few telephone calls. Like Stephen, Manolo makes his *toiles* and then he sends them to John. He recalls the pleasure he had in making the shoes for John's debut couture collection for Dior, shown in January 1997: 'I had such a wonderful time working on it – it was like being on

holiday. I was in Venice and John sent me pictures of the Masai. I was especially excited by the head-dresses, so I decided to adapt them to sandals that would coil up the leg. I rushed around Venice buying all the different tiny beads I could find. Then I made a *toile* and stuck them on it by hand, using UHU glue. Everybody was saying, "You can't do this! It's crazy." But John was very excited and said, "As it's African, what about some fur?"' I said, "Give me some! Some chinchilla!" In the end they looked like naughty little animals, ready to bite!'

It is the fantasy of John Galliano that appeals to Manolo but, as a highly commercial designer, he responds to the fact that, 'underneath all the amazingly

Last minute adjustments from the couturier to ensure that every model looks perfect from top to toe. (Christian Dior prêt-à-porter, autumn/ winter 1997–8, designed by John Galliano photo, above left: B. Gysenberg, Dior archives)

The touch of extravagant *joie-de-vivre* provided by Manolo Blahnik's shoes for Galliano is perfectly captured in the bold stylishness of his drawings, full of dash, wit and style, exactly like Blahnik himself.

beautiful effects the product is always there. Strip away the theatrics and you are left with divine shapes which are not only practical, but very modern.'

It is this practicality which is lost to many critics, blinded by the theatricality of the presentation. Steven Robinson points out that John demands the highest standards in everything, from the flowers to the purely utilitarian production charts for the factories – they have to be beautiful, as well. 'When we do the fittings,' he says, 'we always have in mind what sort of woman would wear the dress. Underneath all the creativity, John is very mathematical and controlled. He keeps reminding me, "Naomi's wearing this or, Claudia is wearing this," and we have to think how to make it so it will help them use their personalities to get it over.'

The same professional practicality animates Galliano's work with both the hairdresser and make-up artists. Odile Gilbert is considered one of the most innovative hairdressers working today. She has created the hair for John's shows for the last three years and she feels that, with the couture and prêt-à-porter collections, they have a continuing all-year-round artistic partnership. 'I have a feeling with him now,' she says. 'I understand him but that doesn't mean he doesn't amaze and delight me. The magic world of Galliano is full of surprises. I get a marvellous charge from him, but also a challenge. I want to do something as good as his clothes. I come in about three weeks before the show. John tells me the story, the fairytale, although I don't see the clothes. I then go and do my research quite independently. I travel all over the world so my stimuli can literally come from anywhere. I can get into John's world because he has the same eye for hair as he has for clothes.'

A week before the show she holds the first of three fittings in her atelier. The first fitting is a general one, using the Galliano-house model, employed for the preliminary fittings of the clothes, where the basic hair story is finalized. The second is a fitting for each individual look, and the last is girl by girl, for each individual dress.

'There's much more to an Odile Gilbert hair fitting than you'd think,' John says. 'She sources human hair from all over the world; has it sewn together in New York, and then sends it to the finest colourist in Paris for it to be bleached, then dyed to the range of colours she's chosen for the show. The process isn't just involved; it is *so* loving. It always upsets Odile when people talk of her making wigs. And she's right – it is so much more. She has an atelier with her own chemicals and sewing machines. It's a costly and time-consuming process with as much scientific creativity as artistic creativity.

Creating the hair for a Galliano show is very much more than a comb-and-hairspray job. Top international hairdresser Odile Gilbert searches the world for inspiration to complement Galliano's ideas and uses techniques ancient and modern to create memorable hairstyles of total originality. (Photo: Anne Deniau, Givenchy archives)

'For the Dior show, the hair was so complicated that Odile had to have her team do the hair for all the magazine fashion shoots. She kept her entire team – which comes from all over the world – in Paris for an extra week and sent them out with each of the magazines. Odile has a large team but they inspire and understand each other. Above all, they understand her and her demands, which is important, as she can't possibly do every girl's hair herself. In many cases all she has to do is check and tweak a bit. Her team is marvellous. They've been coming for years and they still go out and find a McDonald's because they hate French food! We love that!'

Another person who fields a big team and starts working with John in advance of the show is Stéphane Marais, who conceives the make-up. They have worked together for eight years and have total mutual trust. The process starts well in advance with a brief conversation between the two men. From this, Stéphane will begin to have ideas of how the make-up should be, but he prefers to keep his proposals in his head until he has seen the clothes. 'I know what his feelings and inspirations are,' he claims, 'so I know the sort of feeling he wants the make-up to have. The night before, with the final fittings, I stay very late and I like to surprise him – you know, maybe I can see something at the last moment. And John always says, "Do it."'

The day of the show, when all the work, theorizing, research and discussions come to fruition, is a long one. It starts at around seven in the morning, with Steven Robinson and Vanessa arriving at the venue, which they may only have left a few hours before, having worked virtually the entire night through. The next two hours are spent checking every detail of the clothes, making sure that all the accessories are with them and everything is ready to be put on. For a show scheduled at eight in the evening, the first girls will arrive at eight in the morning. The teams of hair and make-up artists begin to work with them. The newer girls arrive early; others are in by about eleven and the supermodels will arrive by two – the very latest time for an evening show. As John Galliano says, 'There's a whole hierarchy thing going on with the girls and the make-up and hair people with which I never get involved. There are too many forces going on. The girls know their moment – when to make eyes at a certain make-up artist. It's all very eighteenth-century, like Versailles. The younger girls are looking and learning. The ones who've been there for ages won't go to Stéphane's seat. They *daren't* take that chair. Naomi will.'

It is a day which flies by. The girls talk, snooze, have their boyfriends and family in, and endlessly telephone. They sit for over an hour while false hair is sewn in – there are no wigs used. They all want Odile's hand and the master make-up touch of Stéphane. In fact, each specialist brings a team of a dozen or more hair and make-up artists. There are considerable numbers behind the scenes by mid-afternoon. fifty girls, each with a dresser, all the make-up and hair artists, security men, pressers, coffee-makers, technicians, family, friends, hangers-on, TV cameras and their crews; the atmosphere becomes sharper, more anticipatory; the mood swings from ordered chaos to controlled partying. Everyone is aware that the feeling must be kept lively if the show is to have the spirit and life to take the audience with it. Theatricality starts long before the show commences.

'We tell the story at the fittings,' John says. 'The whole story, not just the individual girl's part. The walk. The attitudes. They study the dress. They like

137

BLUSH

GIVENCHY PAP OCTOBRE 96

RUSSIAN PRINCESS   ANNA KARENINE
LUCRECIA

John Galliano
Spring Summer 1994

Cour Carrée Du Louvre
Salle Sully
Rue De L'Amiral Coligny
75001 Paris

Friday 08 October. 18h 30

Name ....

....

Block ....

JOHN GALLIANO   SHow à 18h30

RDV à: 13h30   Cour Carrée. Salle Sully.

MANNEQUINS:

MARIE SOPHIE
EMMA WARG
HELENA CHRISTENSEN
LORRAINE
HELENA BAROULLA
HELENA CORDURA
OLGA
KATE MOSS
MICKY
CRISTY
NAOMI
MEGHAN
JAIMIE
DEBBIE DIETERING
NICKY TAYLOR
JANE POWERS
KALIO

Equipe: THIERRY →
JACQUES →
WILLIAMS –
HUÉ LAN
EMMANUEL
OKUBO
MIDORIKO arrivé à 15h40
MOI
ONODA} depart 16h
YUKI

John Galliano
Spring Summer 1994.

Cour Carré Du Lo
Salle Sully

direction but their personalities are really important so I encourage them to interpret it all in a way that is right for them. They find their way. What they can't be is timid. They don't get a second chance. I tell them, "It's your one outfit, honey. You only get one shot! Go for it!" And they know it. They worry terribly.'

During the day, John takes each girl through the rooms for an individual rehearsal. 'Here's a good place to pause.' 'Why don't you lie on that couch for a minute before you go on? The photographers can see you there.' 'Lean against this tree.' It's theatre and John rehearses it to fit each girl's personality. 'They get nervous,' Steven says. 'They are so frightened of letting John down. His method makes many more demands

Stéphane Marais is one of the world's leading make-up artists, responsible for the appearance of many of the top Parisian couturiers models. He works with the same painstaking care as Galliano does to ensure that his team is aware of all the historic references behind the make-up he creates to enhance the spirit of each show. (Right, photo: Christian Dior archive)

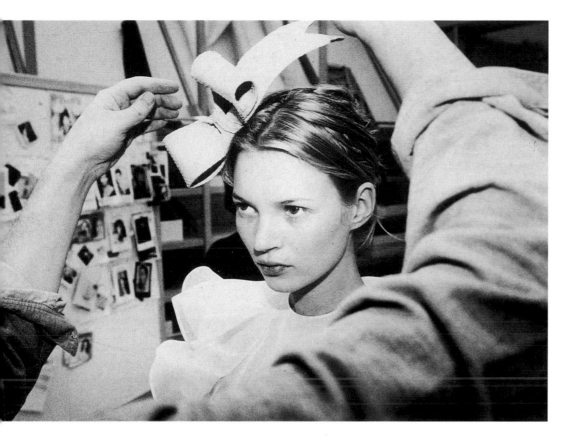

Creating beautiful things is intriguing but, as Kate Moss shows, being fitted for millinery by Stephen Jones is not all sombre seriousness. (Photos: Andrew McPherson)

outfits. This gives everybody time to ensure that every detail is perfect. As each model wears only one outfit, the team all have the luxury of making it a relaxed, jokey affair. Steven Robinson describes the countdown: 'The people who made the patterns are there so they know exactly how everything should be. It's a slow, painstaking process. The shoes have arrived a few days earlier – always perfectly packed and boxed – and Stephen is there, adjusting the hats, which often have to be in place before the hair can be finished. John walks around, checking, chatting and joking, vibing the girls.'

John adds, 'I say to them, "Who do you really want to work with? Sleep with? He's out there tonight. Imagine he's at the end of the room. Do it for him! Do it for me!" Sometimes they do it too much, but that's fun too, because it shows they're not afraid. Can you imagine what it's like for them? How insecure they feel? They shake and tremble. It's terrifying for them. They know the big guns – the top editors, bookers and photographers – are out there. They sometimes lose it just before they go on. They're standing there with napkins under their arms, in case they're sweating. "Oh! I'm going to pass out!" My job is to keep up their energy: "You look fabulous! You look heaven! You're beautiful! Do that shape again! That's fabulous! Don't lose it!"

'Then, everything has been done. There are no last minute ribbons to tie or buttons to fasten. We have final checks. Steven takes some of the girls. So does Bill. I'll take about fifteen. Five minutes before it starts, the atmosphere is fab. People are screaming and shouting. We're all burning up energy. Checking! Checking! Working on their characters. Then "Go for it! This is your chance! Lay it on!"'

than traditional shows because he gives them scope to *be* the character, the woman in the dress.' But they love it because they know they have a role. A John Galliano show is not a catwalk – it's stage – and, like any theatrical experience it is quite demanding. They are not just walking down and back; they are acting. There is a lot to remember. They are in front of the audience, without the respite of going behind the scenes to change, for a considerable time. It is, in the widest sense of the word, exposure.

The rehearsal with John is crucial. As Stephen Jones put it, 'If she is to perform well, a model must be wound up like a spring before a show, and it is John who gives her the energy to keep going.' One hour before the show, every girl is dressed. In most fashion shows the models have anything from four to eight changes of clothes, but Galliano prefers to show fewer

Behind the scenes, the goddesses of high glamour become real people again and enjoy some of the more earthly pleasures. (Photo: Andrew McPherson)

'It's hype! hype! hype!' says Steven. 'They're the ones who will sell us,' John adds. 'They make the industry go round.' To John's cries of 'Shape! Shape! Shape!' the models step out and begin to tell the story.

In common with all fashion shows, Galliano collections run late, not, as some of the more naïve fashion journalists believe, deliberately to hype up the audience or – an opinion even more bizarre, yet often expressed – in order to humble the professionals waiting on the other side of the curtain, but because the slightest hitch has ramifications with considerable effects behind the scenes. A model arrives late – a make-up artist calls in sick – the sound system is temperamental – and there is an immediate knock-on effect which, potentially, can delay proceedings by anything up to an hour. It is even worse if these things happen in earlier shows during the day as, once lost, it is almost impossible to regain the ground.

A late show causes tension in the audience, which can lead to a frustrated slow handclap – usually initiated by the cameramen, who have arrived at the venue long before the other guests and, of course, must stand and wait while the rest are seated. The first few girls to appear have a formidable task, breaking down any hostility and animating and energizing the flagging spirits of the audience while focusing its attention on the clothes.

The show takes less than thirty minutes. It is over far too soon for the journalists, torn between scribbling in their notepads or making quick rudimentary sketches as an *aide-mémoire*, and the compelling necessity to keep looking, so that nothing is missed. In a Galliano show, the layers of reference, the plethora of detail and the subtleties of cut and colour, quite apart from the beauty and drama of the clothes, can beat even the most practised. Dresses that would repay ten minutes' study and still not reveal all whisk in front of the audience and are gone in less than five.

Nevertheless, even at that speed, the highly trained eyes of experienced journalists catch not only the mood of the collection but a remarkable amount of its detail with considerable accuracy. The most important aspect of their job is identification. They must differentiate between what is new and what is a development from previous collections, while capturing for their readers the overall cultural feeling of the show. Then they must recreate the mood in prose as purple as their editors will permit, prose that flatters the readers by assuming they have knowledge of the cultural allusions used, prose that is a clever form of self-aggrandizement for the journalist who is making the allusions. If there is a Chinese element, for example, as there has been recently in several of Galliano's collections, it is not enough merely to say so. There must be literary

allusions – Pearl S. Buck, or, even better, Somerset Maugham. There must be historic references – the Boxer Rebellion is a well-worn favourite. And, to bring it down to earth so that *all* readers can 'get the picture', references to Suzy Wong and even Madame Butterfly are acceptable.

The world of the fashion correspondent is a hysterical and uncertain one. It is governed by taste – a notoriously slippery and unreliable concept. It is because there are no fixed rules that praise frequently becomes not only extravagant but hyperbolic. Words change meanings. Absolutes and superlatives abound. And, beneath it all, lies a deadening sense of futility,

fatuity and shallowness. Fashion journalists can say the silliest things without the slightest blush of embarrassment, but some at least are able to laugh at their more extreme foolishness. Charles Gandee, writing in American *Vogue* 'from the taffeta-lined trenches of the fashion department' described a 'fashion moment' for his readers: 'Someone will hold up a John Galliano bias-cut silk dress, fresh off the plane from Paris… and ten thin young women in black clothes will instantly stop what they're doing, fling themselves on the garment, and shriek and gasp and clutch their breasts as if their hearts were about to explode. And then… they all scream "Fabulous!"' One

There is an Edwardian extravagance in the items required to ensure that every model is looking her magnificent best before she steps out before the most critical audience in the world. (Photos: Andrew McPherson)

wishes that Mark Twain were alive and reporting fashion today.

Of course, plaudits are one thing, sales quite another. The continuing debate in fashion circles about whether dress-designing is art, craft or pure commerce arises because dress in the abstract has little meaning for the majority of us. We may visit costume exhibitions — including those devoted to contemporary work — with eyes and minds attuned to viewing and assessing the items on display as works of art, but no designer can survive if that is the *only* way in which his creations are viewed. His business continues only through sales. If they slump, so does he. Whereas most artists are

one-man bands, able to make the decision on a purely individual level to continue in the face of public indifference and facing whatever privations that decision brings, no dress designer is in that position. They are all employers, in a way that few artists are. They must make money in order to pay their workforce, even if they are personally prepared to 'starve for their art'.

Selling is the crucial bottom line to the weeks of work which are put into a collection. In many fashion houses, sales are almost entirely completed before the show; in others, the buyers prefer to wait until they've seen the show before committing themselves to specific orders.

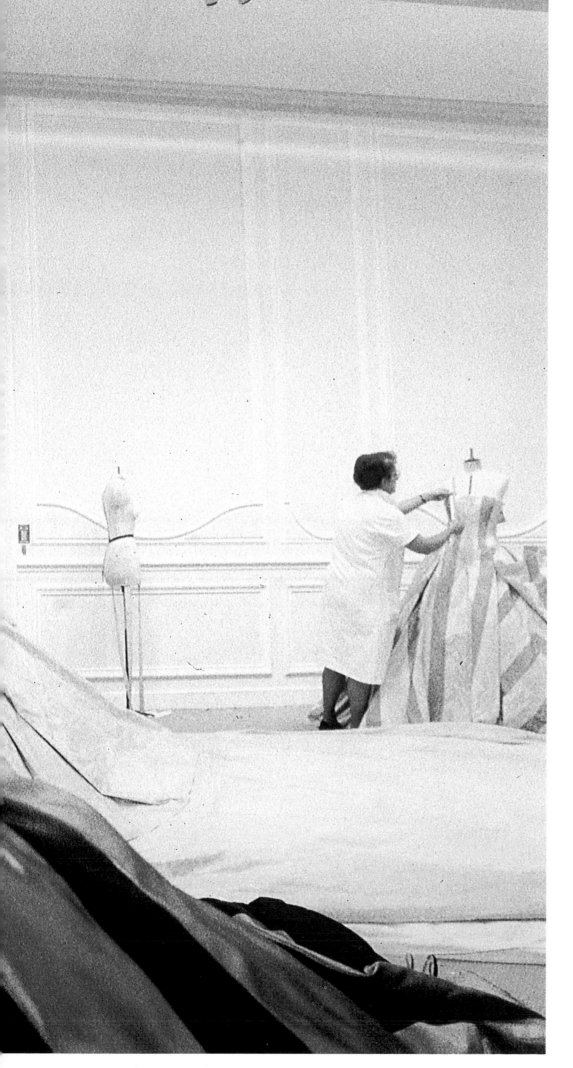

They want to understand fully the season's story, and they feel that it is with the show and how the clothes are styled that they can comprehend the thrust of what the designer is saying and note where he places most emphasis. Only then do they feel they can make an informed choice of garments, which they in their turn must be able to sell.

Certainly, the show is a selling tool and that is what justifies its considerable cost. A medium-sized fashion show can easily cost over £150,000; a Galliano-style show can even more easily top double that amount. That is why it cannot be used merely as a designer's self-indulgence. Everything in it must serve a purpose and justify its cost. And if, on the following day, the designer and his team are poring eagerly over the first of the newspaper reports, the accountants, business associates (and probably the designer too) are equally, if not more, interested in the sales figures.

Following a good collection, the day after the show, the showroom is under siege. After the Galliano presentation in São Schlumberger's mansion in 1993, created in the face of bankruptcy and with no proper business plan in place, Galliano and his team were horrified as much as delighted by the instant response. With a minute staff, it meant that everybody had to be

Grandeur and extravagance for John Galliano's first couture show for the house of Givenchy; as final adjustments are made behind the scenes to a series of magnificently scaled ballgowns, one of which is worn here by Steven Robinson's assistant Vanessa Bellanger. (Photo: Andrew McPherson)

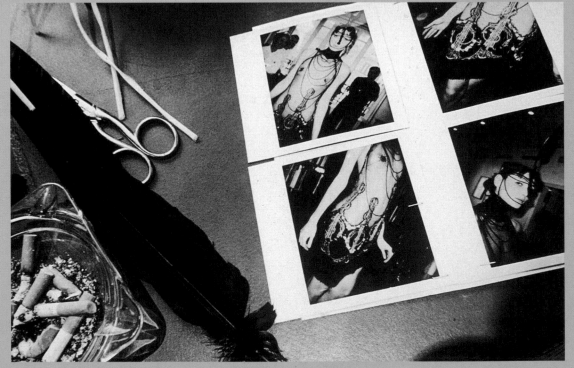

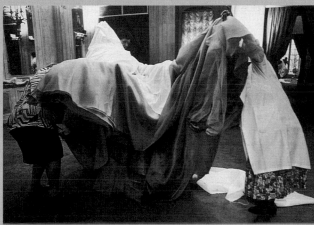

called in to help cope with demand. The press officer was sorting out pricing; John was doing the selling; his assistant was organizing confirmations with the shops and, in between, they were all frantically laying the patterns out on any space available throughout the mansion, grading them for size to enable the factory to get some sort of production going to begin satisfying the demands.

For a few days, the Schlumberger *hôtel particulier* was the Galliano headquarters, until a suitable space was found in the Passage du Cheval Blanc. The Galliano headquarters were up two flights of twisting stairs, in a very cramped space, but at least they were a proper space that could be permanently organized. The showroom was at the end of the cul-de-sac, and it was to be here that women made their pilgrimage: Nan Kempner, Anne Bass, and all the rich and

fashionable women who are the backbone of high fashion have picked their way along the cobbles, past the parked cars, abandoned furniture and overflowing dustbins.

Galliano redecorates his showroom every season in the spirit of his current collection. Its last manifestation was Egyptian, the walls giving the impression of the inside of a royal tomb. Galliano's increased business in the last few seasons meant that Passage du Cheval Blanc became impossibly over-pressurized; in May 1997 the firm moved to a disused doll factory in rue d'Avron, designed to give everyone adequate office space and a large showroom – luxuries that the designer has been forced to do without in the past. Most importantly, the new headquarters are able to cope with post-show pressures much better than previously.

One of the major necessities is to accommodate the

demands of fashion shoots, which begin after the show. Whereas many European magazines will not make the final choice of garments they wish to feature for a little while, the all-important American ones tend to photograph very soon after the show, in order to take advantage of the fact that the top hair and make-up artists, as well as the major photographers, are in Paris for only a limited time. Juggling the needs of the top magazines so that they all get what they want without attracting cries of favouritism is a delicate task, demanding tact, finesse and a cool head.

But it is an essential one. How a fashion magazine chooses to photograph its choices from a collection is of great concern to a designer, not only because those photographs will set the tone for the magazine's readers of what he has tried to do. It will also confirm

'John is the greatest stylist of all time. He has an incredible eye.'

— AMANDA HARLECH

— or otherwise — what the designer felt were the important and directional items in the show. The conformity of choice might well make outsiders think of collusion but, in fact, the reason three or four dresses from each season appear in all the magazines is that they are the ones that encapsulate the designer's statement. And, although designers are by no means always happy about how the photographers, stylists and editors project their look, they always closely scrutinize the published pictures, knowing that, regardless of what they may feel, it is the image on the page that will set the tone for the public.

Balenciaga used to begin to select his fabrics for his next collection on the day of his press show. Few designers are so obsessed today. All take a break as soon as possible after the show. John Galliano normally goes

away for a week, to do nothing more onerous than lie on a beach in the sun and unwind. When he comes back, the creative process starts all over again. Ideas he has been mulling over, sources not used or fully developed previously, are revisited. Possible leads begin to sprout like tender green plants pushing through the winter soil. The search is on for the idea, the story, the spirit of the next collection with which the designer will make his statement to the world. It is a search that becomes more demanding with each consecutive success; a search made increasingly difficult by media and retail expectations of consistency of vision which must be retained while satisfying the need for novelty every six months. How to balance such apparently mutually exclusive demands is the great conundrum for fashion designers in the late twentieth century.

'Energy is what gives beauty to an idea'

IV

PARIS:
'Some Inventive Madness'

C REATIVELY, PARIS IS THE most accommodating of all Europe's cities, welcoming artists from around the globe and affording them the tolerance and freedom to find their own fulfillment. It is especially open to fashion designers. Charles Frederick Worth, considered the father of modern couture, was an Englishman who arrived in the city in 1845 and eventually became the world's most famous couturier.

In this century, it was to Paris that the Italian, Schiaparelli; the American, Mainbocher; and the Irishman, Molyneux; came to make their names. Most famously, it was to Paris that Balenciaga, arguably the greatest couturier since Worth, turned after London had rejected him in the late thirties when he was looking for sanctuary from the Spanish Civil War. And it was to Paris that John Galliano looked for a future that seemed increasingly unlikely to be safeguarded in London.

A timeless study of the beauty of John Galliano's vision of femininity, in his spring/summer 1994 collection. (Photo: David Seidner)

Galliano's move to Paris released a nw creative force in him, as his work became increasingly complex in cut and scale: fabrics acted and reacted against each other to produce a unity which, despite its apparent simplicity, was a marvellously controlled exercise in dressmaking at its highest point. (Drawings by Julie Verhoeven from Galliano's autumn/winter 1994–5 collection)

The many faces of Galliano glamour show how wide a creative spectrum he works within. Although there are many different moods in these clothes, they all share one thing: complete artistic authority.

Clockwise from top left: Galliano, spring/summer 1994 (Niall McInerney); Galliano, spring/summer 1993 (Patrice Stable Agency); Galliano, spring/summer 1996 (both Niall McInerney). This page, below: Galliano, spring/summer 1995 (Niall McInerney); opposite: Gallliano spring/summer 1995. (Niall McInery)

Evening glamour takes many forms, from the exotically bouffant to the slinkily clinging, but whether it is a question of controlling many yards of material, or cutting on the bias a dress which highlights every nuance of the figure, Galliano has mastered both skills. (Photos: Patrick Demarchelier)

John Galliano's forte is the bias-cut satin dress. No one has done it better since Mme Vionnet first invented the technique in the 1920s. This deceptively simple but consummate example of the art is worn by Linda Evangelista, and is from the Galliano spring/summer 1994 collection. (Photo: Steven Meisel)

The thing which makes Paris unique in the world's fashion capitals is not only the range and nationality of its designers but also its infrastructure of craftsmanship, without which work to the highest level of couture is impossible. It is in Paris that the fingers of the cleverest workers in feathers and beading are found. The manufacturers of buttons and trims reach a standard there that can be found nowhere else. It is this city alone that produces the most exquisite ribbons in colours bolder or more subtle than those found elsewhere. Paris is the city which can turn the most far-fetched designer fantasy into reality. It was this city which was to revitalize John Galliano with its attitudes and give him hope for his future.

John was no stranger to Paris. He had held his first show there in 1989 and had already been selling there in order to reach a wider audience. 'I was ready for it,' he recalls. 'It was an adventure. I had contacts here and, of course, Steven came with me.' Steven Robinson adds, 'We already had a press officer in Paris. So, we thought, what should John do to get over to Paris? We were prepared to go backwards and forwards until we found backers but the move happened virtually overnight. London was dead. Nothing was happening. John said, "We're moving." And we did. Faycal believed in John and he made it all possible.' 'I knew I'd stay,' John continues. 'I was committed to Paris. I knew that I could make my dreams come true there.'

Faycal Amor faced John's problems head on, with instant practicality. As the designer-owner of the Plein

Sud sportswear label, he was able to provide backing: a public relations organization and a computerized clothing factory, where it was planned to manufacture Galliano's Girl, the casual, jeans-based range that had first been mooted when John was at Aguecheek. Amanda Harlech saw a difference very quickly. 'John was able to develop new techniques because the Plein Sud factory had marvellously sophisticated machinery and a highly technical staff. They had faggoting machines which produced amazingly delicate work. It was marvellous for John. He was able to use really good fabrics for the first time in his career. Things like leather and brocade. But it came with a price-tag. Suddenly design integrity was less of a teeth-grinding issue than production, it seemed to me.'

John points out, 'I learned a lot from Faycal. He was so practical. He showed me how to secure my labels – although there were complications with that, as he gave his address on the documents – and he taught me about mass manufacture. At the end of the day, Galliano's Girl didn't catch on. The price difference between it and the main range was too small, people went for the real thing. It turned Galliano into a house with two heads.'

Galliano's first Paris show in 1989, immediately after Aguecheek had pulled out, had been a shoestring affair. 'We had literally to make the collection out of paper,' Amanda Harlech told US *Vogue*. But, under Amor's umbrella, things loosened up a lot. John's studio consisted of eight people who did everything, including taking time to do the washing-up and Hoovering.

Despite the artistic success of his collections, difficulties with his backer meant that, by 1993, John was alone again with only his team to support him. He slept on friends' floors and he borrowed money for the Métro. But that didn't worry him in the least. He looks back and says philosophically, 'My life has all been twists and turns but it's had its moments – magic moments.' What really hurt him after parting company with Amor was that he was unable to stage a show. Even now, in his success, it pains him: 'I missed a season, and that was terrible.'

But the magic moments were to return. 'We'd made quite an impact with the Olivia Philibustier show for Spring–Summer 1993, especially in America. Anna Wintour, editor-in-chief of American *Vogue*, and André Leon Talley, *Vanity Fair*'s European correspondent, became great fans. I'd reached the point where I wanted my independence, to have my own house. People knew that I was deadly serious and that I wouldn't go on working as I was. I was seeing various people about backing, including Italians.' It was after a trip to Milan that he had dinner with Anna Wintour, who was appalled by the situation he was in.

Editors of great fashion magazines are not always renowned for gentleness or sentimentality. They are generally considered one of the tougher sub-species of *Homo sapiens*. But what they all share is not just a shrewd fashion judgement, a response to beauty and a respect for talent, but also an ability to judge a situation practically, and to take action. Anna Wintour was no exception.

Her advice was crisp and incontrovertible. 'You cannot miss another season. You must do something,' she urged. To John it seemed madness. There were four weeks before the collections. He had no studio and no money. But he knew she was right. What he perhaps didn't know is that the path to editor-in-chief of a major magazine is no primrose-strewn country lane. It is the hardest, most dangerous *autostrada* in the world. It makes the person who successfully negotiates it not only determined but resourceful. The Wintour rescue operation began that night.

Firstly, she did what powerful women usually do to start the ball rolling: she arranged a lunch. André Leon Talley took John to meet São Schlumberger, a Portuguese socialite, for what was to be the first of what became known as the 'staff lunches' with her at which, John recalls, she served fantastic Portuguese sardines. André asked her if she might be prepared to lend her eighteenth-century *hôtel particulier* as a venue for a show. She had already bought from Galliano and was a devoted follower of couture, having consistently patronized Givenchy, Dior and Chanel in the past. Even so, her answer surprised John. 'Yes, why not?' she responded straight away.

It was the turning point. From that show on, held in the empty mansion which had been up for sale for some time, no Galliano collection would ever be shown in humdrum or predictable surroundings again. But before the show could take place, a backer needed to be found. Anna Wintour arranged for John to be flown

The quintessential Romantic ballgown by Galliano for Givenchy: Monumental yet fluid, it is high fashion at its traditional best. (Photo: Lillian Bassman)

For autumn/winter 1996–7, Galliano turned to native American patterned blankets for inspiration, using their bold blocks of colour to create clothes unlike any previously seen in Paris: naïve yet sophisticated, strong but subtle. (Photo: Max Vadukul)

Right: Cartoon by the photographer Bruce Weber of John Galliano during the designer's time at Givenchy.

to New York in order to meet the right people. As John recalls, his close friend André was with him 'pushing and pushing. I met Anne Bass who took me to the premier of *Schindler's List* and introduced me to all her girlfriends, including Nan Kempner. There were little dinners, smart lunches. I kept thinking, "What are you *doing* here, John?"'

At one dinner he sat next to Donald B. Marron, Chairman and Chief Executive Officer of the investment bank Paine Webber International. On his return to Paris he had a phone call from Anna Wintour telling him to meet a man called John Bult at the Bristol Hotel who was in Europe with his colleague Mark Rice. They were from Paine Webber. André Leon Talley joined them with, in John's words, 'a set of fantastic pictures shot by the top fashion photographer Steven Meisel of Linda Evangelista. For once in my life, the pictures had been shot to look commercial – not Dotty Duchess dresses but, like, that silk jersey dress you have to have now. RIGHT now! André said, "This is how much *Vogue* thinks of this guy – and he needs help." The reply was, "What do you need?"'

It was to be one of the most extraordinary shows Paris had ever seen – not so much a comeback as a statement of future promise. With only fifteen days to go it was decided to do only seventeen outfits, but on seventeen 'of the most beautiful women in the world'. The Schlumberger mansion had been empty and up for sale for some time. John decided to let this set the mood for the show. 'We opened windows, brought in tons of dead leaves to scatter around, filled fallen chandeliers with rose petals, created unmade beds and carefully placed

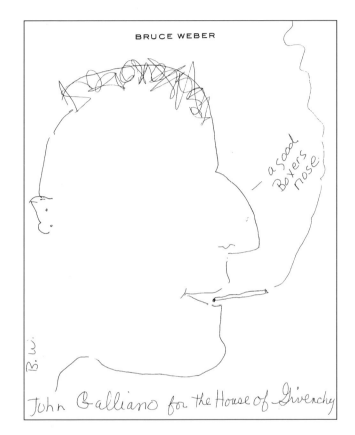

BRUCE WEBER

a good Boxers nose

B.W.

John Galliano for the House of Givenchy

upturned chairs at various points. We filled the house with dry ice so that the whole place had a desolate, poetic look, like a Sarah Moon photograph. We lit the house from outside to give it an early morning dew feel. The girls worked the whole house from the top floor down. It was like an old salon presentation. Gorgeous creatures with heavenly, heady make-up wandering through this deserted house, bending down and looking for abandoned love letters in the dust… it was magic.'

The invitation was a rusty key with a handwritten label attached to it, but the scenes in the courtyard were bedlam as hundreds of gate-crashers tried to force their way in. 'It was a "moment",' Galliano concedes. 'A lot of people thought it was all very cleverly contrived and

Previous page: The way in which a dress is shown on the catwalk is evolved in rehearsals by the interaction of the personalities of the designer, the model and the dress. Givenchy haute couture, spring/ summer 1996, designed by John Galliano. (Photos: Andrew McPherson)

The ethereal recreation of the quality of an Ingres painting may, at first glance, make this dress appear almost like a costume, until the eye notices the complex beauty of the tiny jacket, which is totally modern and uniquely Galliano. (Galliano, spring/summer 1994; photo: David Seidner)

then up in the special lift to the top floor. There I was ushered into a huge room. There was one big table and all that was on it was a bottle of mineral water and two glasses. Suddenly there was this amazingly elegant figure in grey. He had very strong, young eyes and controlled, small movements. I showed him my research books and explained how I worked. My hair was long – I had dreadlocks then – and I had to keep trying to press it down. I was impressed with how well he had been briefed. He knew everything already.'

What Arnault was most interested in knowing was how Galliano would sustain interest after the first two collections, when the novelty had gone. 'I talked about finding the identifiable moments in Givenchy's career. Once the meeting had started, I relaxed. I knew this was just a formality. I'd already been checked out and I'd met all of the Givenchy hierarchy. People had been giving Galliano the once-over for weeks, checking deliveries, the quality of the work and everything to make sure we

weren't a flaky prospect. They were *very* thorough.' The appointment was announced in July 1995.

Galliano has since wondered if Givenchy was already seen by Arnault as a rehearsal for Dior. If it was, no hint was given at the meeting which finalized the deal, and John started immediately by looking closely at Givenchy's career, searching for 'moments', although he couldn't use the archives until Givenchy had actually left. Although he fully understands the sensibility of Christian Dior, he found it much more difficult to identify answering chords in Givenchy. 'But I was basically so happy just to have the set-up to work within, to be able to do couture, that I knew it would be all right. I had to learn to work within the Givenchy structure. I'd never been in a couture establishment before, let alone been in charge of one. But the people in the ateliers were marvellous.' Hubert de Givenchy had been an old-style couturier, very formal and dignified. He wore the traditional white overall when

Evening glamour can be on a lavishly eighteenth-century scale or as delicate as a filigree shawl from the belle époque. In either case, it is their total femininity which gives these dresses their appeal. Left and right: Givenchy haute couture, spring/summer 1996, designed by John Galliano. (Photos: B. Pellerin, Givenchy archive)

working, but always beneath it was a city suit and an immaculately knotted tie. He kept a distance between himself and the atelier staff. Galliano broke that tradition on the first day by eating in the staff canteen. 'Lentils and fish – and sixty pairs of eyes on me!' he recalls. And, of course, his dress codes were notoriously free and easy.

The pressing need was to make the Givenchy line look younger. It seemed to Galliano that Givenchy's approach was too couture-dictated, even in his ready-to-wear. 'He was temperamentally always designing with his private customers in mind. He just didn't have a prêt-à-porter angle. The clothes had to be given a broader appeal for the shops.' But before that could be tackled, there was a couture collection to be designed, to be shown in January 1996, and the Galliano collection to be prepared for the October 1995 Paris shows.

The Galliano show was held at the Théâtre des Champs Elysées, famous as the venue for the Ballets Russes in 1913, and the scandal of *Le Sacre du Printemps*, which was premiered there. Galliano's staging exploited the theatrical possibilities of the space by placing members of the audience on stage, including Paloma Picasso, Inès de la Fressange, Azzadine Alaïa and Gianfranco Ferré, and having the models move

Galliano, autumn/winter 1995–6. (Photos: Patrice Stable Agency)

Galliano, spring/summer 1993. (Photos: Patrice Stable Agency)

among the guests in the auditorium. The overall theme was a ballet school at rehearsal time. As *The New York Times* described it, 'There was a ballet bar with prepubescent ballerinas doing *pliés* in front of a mirror, a make-up table cluttered with wadded Kleenexes, a woman with a *pince-nez* playing the piano, stacked wicker baskets exploding with tulle,' and, drifting through it all were clothes which *Women's Wear Daily* called, 'the most exquisite anyone has seen in Paris this season… He can do the most elaborate taffeta ballgowns or the simplest black pelmet jacket… and make them look like no other designer's – before or

now.' As the *New York Times* said, 'It had the sort of edge that propelled Mr Galliano to authority…' – an authority which had brought him the award of British Designer of the Year for a third, unprecedented, time and Spain's most prestigious fashion accolade, *Telva* magazine's Designer of the Year Award, both in 1995.

It was this authority which Bernard Arnault was expecting in January 1996. He nearly didn't get a Givenchy couture show at all, as Paris was paralysed by an eighteen-day strike shortly before the shows. 'It was a nightmare,' Galliano recalls. 'The women in the ateliers had to walk to work. Paris was one huge traffic

High-gloss glamour revisited. John Galliano's reworking of the world of 1950s chic conjures visions of the elegant creations of Dior, Fath and Balmain, as worn by the models of the time, Suzy Parker and Lisa Fonssagrives. Galliano spring/summer 1995. (Photos: Mario Testino)

'He is a perfectionist because he knows no other way. It has nothing to do with money. When he had no money, it was exactly the same. Getting everything perfect is much more important to him than eating or having a bed to sleep in. He could never cut corners for such trivial things.'

— STEPHEN JONES

into the world looking as perfect as a showhorse. Critics of Galliano sometimes say that the woman who wears his clothes is equally unimportant to him.

Charles James, seen by most fashion historians as, at the least, the technical equal of Balenciaga, viewed his customers as enemies who were always wanting to take away his creations before they were 'ready'. An obsessive perfectionist, he *never* felt they were ready. He was always convinced that the more time spent, the better the result — to use the term 'end product' would be inappropriate to a man who never contemplated an end. Eccentric, litigious, famously quarrelsome, Charles James was one of the greatest fashion experimenters of the century, working out the principles of cut and movement in fabric by an intricate series of calculations more akin to engineering than to

the work of most fashion designers — calculations that would be entirely understood by John Galliano.

Galliano need be compared only with the greats of twentieth-century fashion, for that is what he has already proved that he will be. In fact, most fashion followers say that he has reached his level of excellence already. Certainly, there is a constancy in his work which suggests a creative maturity. Diverse, experimental, innovative and able to use history to his own ends, he combines the imaginative prodigality and the technical austerity of the very best of the past. The John Galliano of the nineties has grown, deepened and developed from the Galliano of the eighties. He seems set to enter the twenty-first century with the same energy, dedication and determination that, regardless of setbacks, he has shown in his career to date.

Glamour Preserved: ball gowns in protective dress bags, ready for their next appearance. (Photo: François-Marie Banier)

'I've been lucky all the way. Lots work hard and don't make it.'

— JOHN GALLIANO

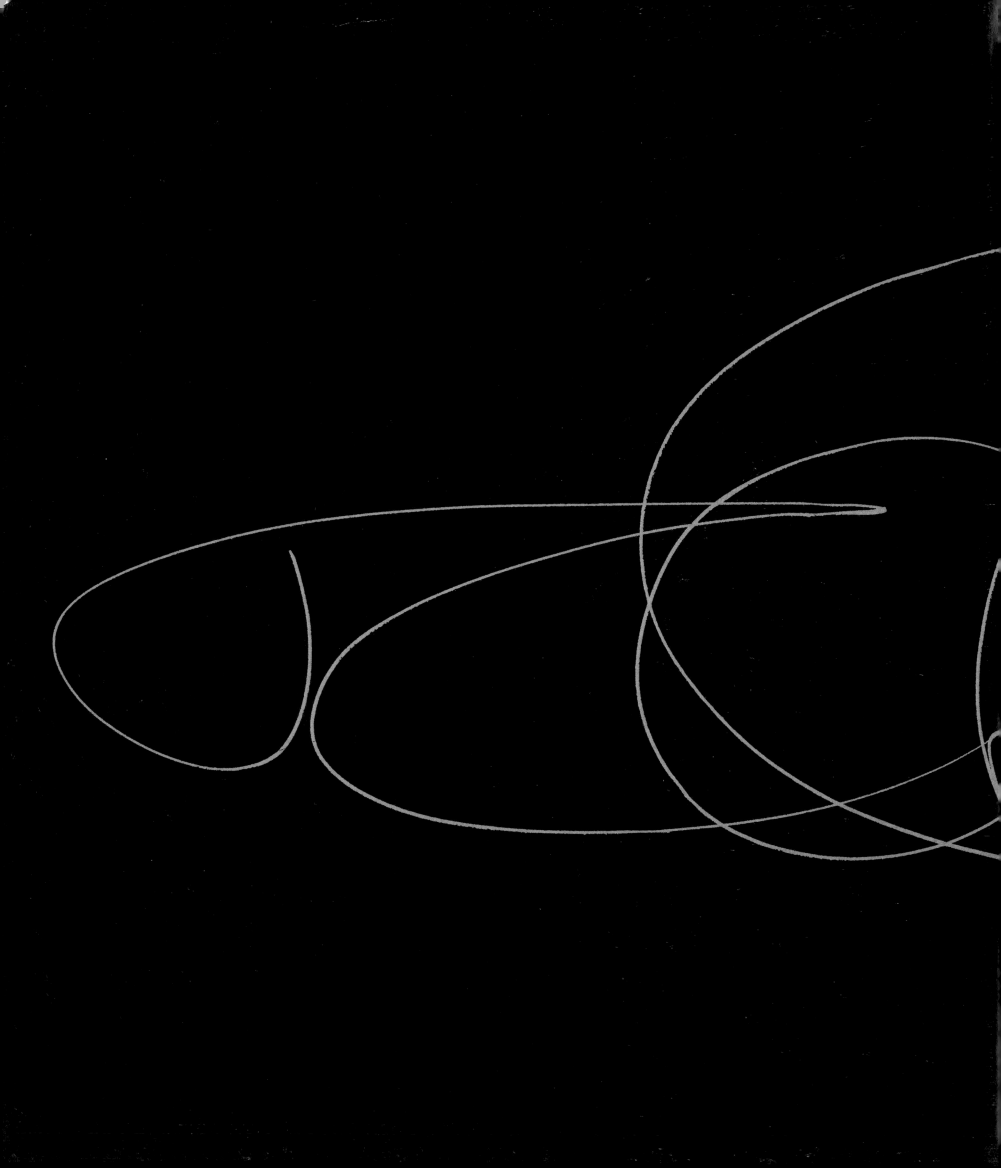